To: _____

From: _____

Date: _____

The Bible
Illustrated
for
Little Children

The Bible
Illustrated
for
Little Children

by
ELLA K. LINDVALL

Illustrated by
PAUL TURNBAUGH

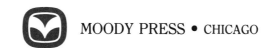
MOODY PRESS • CHICAGO

Library of Congress Cataloging-in-Publication Data

Lindvall, Ella K.
  The Bible illustrated for little children.

  Summary: Brief versions of 183 Bible stories from
both the Old and New Testaments with questions for
discussion.
  1. Bible stories, English.   2. Bible — Illustrations.
[1. Bible stories]   I. Title.
BS551.2.L47   1985   220.9′505   85-18940
ISBN 0-8024-0596-7

1 2 3 4 5 6 7 Printing/DP/Year 90 89 88 87 86 85

OTHER BOOKS BY ELLA K. LINDVALL:

Read-Aloud Bible Stories, vol. 1   *Joseph and His Brothers*
Read-Aloud Bible Stories, vol. 2   *Joseph and the King*
The Birth of Jesus   *The Lost Son and Other Stories*
Jesus Begins His Work   *Miracles by the Sea*
Jonah and the Great Fish   *Noah and His Ark*

Printed in the United States of America

It is always a pleasure for me to see a new book of Bible stories for young children. "Give me a child until he is five years old," the saying goes, "and his life pattern will then be set for good or ill." I believe this to be generally true. Moody Press is to be commended for this new addition to their splendid line of children's books.

KENNETH N. TAYLOR

Long ago, before there was a beautiful world, God thought about making one. He thought of how the hills would look. And the grass. And the apple trees. And the little streams of water. And the wide oceans. And the dandelions. And the warm sun. And the moon. And the twinkly stars. He thought of them all. And then God started to make things. He made light. And sky. And water. He said, "Let there be dry land," and there it was. He said, "Let the grass grow," and up from the ground it came. He put the sun in the sky. And the moon. And the twinkly stars. God made them all, and He made them all by Himself.

QUESTIONS:

1. *Who thought about making the world?*
2. *Who was strong enough to make it?*
3. *Who helped Him?*
4. *What will God make to live in His world?*

Genesis 1:3-19

ook at what has happened in God's beautiful
world. It is not empty anymore. Something is
walking. What is it? Something is eating. What is it?
Something is flying. What is it? God has filled up His
world with wonderful things that can walk and run and
hop and swim and crawl and fly. Now God will make
one more thing before He is finished. God is going to
make people. He will make Adam, the man. Then He
will make Eve, the lady. Adam and Eve will be the first
people to live in God's beautiful world.

QUESTIONS:

1. *How did the animals get into God's world?*
2. *How did the birds get into God's world?*
3. *How did Adam and Eve get into God's world?*

Genesis 1:20-27

See that fruit in Eve's hand? A while ago God said, "Eat all the fruit you want. Just don't take any from that one special tree." Now Satan, a bad angel, heard what God said. Satan didn't want Adam and Eve to please God. So Satan hid inside a snake and talked to Eve. He said, "It's all right to eat that special fruit." Now Satan was lying. But Eve listened to him. She thought the fruit looked good. She took some off the tree. Now she will eat it. Then she will give some to Adam. See him coming? They both will do what God said not to do. Satan will be glad. But not Adam and Eve. They will be afraid.

QUESTIONS:

1. Who said to leave the special fruit alone?
2. Who said to go ahead and eat it?
3. How will Adam and Eve feel after they have done wrong?

Genesis 3:1-10

See how hard Adam and Eve are working. They aren't in the beautiful garden anymore. They are in another garden. Weeds grow here. Prickly thorns grow here. And it takes a lot of work to make the corn and beans grow. What has happened? Adam and Eve would not do what God told them. So they had to leave the beautiful garden. Now they must work hard to get enough food to eat. But do you see what they are wearing? God has made them clothes from animal skins. Adam and Eve can't go back into the beautiful garden. They have to work hard. But does God still love Adam and Eve? Yes, He does.

QUESTIONS:

1. Why aren't Adam and Eve in the beautiful garden anymore?
2. How do you know God still loves them?

Genesis 3:17-23

12

This kind old man is Enoch. See him standing at the door of his house? Enoch has lived for a long time. He is a daddy, and he is a grandpa. Best of all, Enoch is one of God's friends. Every day Enoch thinks about God. Every day Enoch tries to do what is right. He knows that pleases God. Every day Enoch walks with God, just like a friend. Some day God will say, "Enoch, My friend, come along home with Me." And Enoch will go.

QUESTIONS:

1. *What was the old man's name?*
2. *What did he do every day?*
3. *What pleases God?*

Genesis 5:18-24

13

Abram and Sarai are packing their clothes. They are packing their kitchen things. They are getting ready to move to a faraway place. A while ago God said, "Abram, I want you to leave this place. Come, live in the place I will show you." Abram didn't say, "I am too old to move." Abram didn't say, "I don't want to move." Abram just said, "Sarai, we will do what God says." Soon Abram and Sarai will be ready. Then they will get on their camels and go *plip plop, plip plop* over the sand to their new home.

QUESTIONS:

1. *What is the name of the man?*
2. *Why are Abram and Sarai packing?*
3. *What animals will they ride on?*
4. *Who will show them where to go?*

Genesis 12:1-5

Remember Abram? Here he is in his new country. And here are some of his friends. Look at them go! You see, Abram is Lot's uncle. And Abram has just heard some bad news about Lot. Some soldiers have taken away Lot and many other people. Abram and his helpers will chase after the bad men fast. God gave Abram camels to ride on. God gave Abram helpers. God gave Abram friends. Now God will make Abram strong. He will chase away the bad men and bring Lot home.

QUESTIONS:

1. *Who needs Abram to help him?*
2. *Who gave Abram his camels and friends and helpers?*
3. *Who will help Abram bring Lot home?*

Genesis 14:8-16

15

It is a hot day. The lady and her boy, Ishmael, have been walking through a dry, rocky place. See the boy resting under that bush? The lady doesn't know where they are. But God knows. When they left home this morning they took along bread and some water. But now the water is all gone. The lady doesn't know where to find more water. But God knows. Ishmael is crying because he is so thirsty. The lady cries too. There are no people to hear them. But God hears them. Now He will help the lady see something she hasn't seen before. It is a well of cool water. She will give Ishmael a drink, and he will feel better.

QUESTIONS:

1. *Why is the boy crying?*
2. *What will his mother do for him?*
3. *Who helped her find the water?*

Genesis 21:14-20

One day Abraham is sitting in the doorway of his tent. See him there? Now he looks up. He sees three men coming! Abraham will run to meet them. "Oh, please, do stop at my tent. Rest under the tree, and I will bring some bread." Now these three visitors aren't really men at all. They are really the Lord and two angels! But Abraham doesn't know that yet. And he doesn't know that the Lord is going to tell him some very good news. Abraham will hurry into the tent. "Sarah, Sarah, make some bread!" He will call one of his workers. "Quick, quick, cook some meat!" After supper the Lord will say, "Abraham, Sarah is going to have a baby boy. It will happen next year." Now Abraham and Sarah have wanted a baby boy for a long time. Sarah just can't believe such good news. But she should. When God says something will happen, you can be sure it will. God never tells a lie.

QUESTIONS:

1. *Who is coming to visit Abraham?*
2. *What good news will the Lord tell Abraham?*
3. *Why can we always believe what God says?*

Genesis 18:1-14

God promised to give Abraham and Sarah something. Do you remember what it was? And God always does what He says He will do. See what Sarah is holding? She's holding the baby God has given her. He is soft and cuddly. He has beautiful little hands and feet. He has bright eyes that look this way and that way. He has dark hair. And he cries. Abraham and Sarah love him. Abraham says, "We shall name him Isaac." Do you know what God is doing? He is making a family for the Lord Jesus. Baby Isaac will grow up to be Jesus' great-great-ever-so-great grandpa.

QUESTIONS:

1. *Why were Abraham and Sarah happy?*
2. *Who had promised to give them a baby?*
3. *What was the baby's name?*
4. *Who would be in Isaac's family some day?*

Genesis 21:1-3

What an exciting day! A king has come to visit Abraham. He is the one wearing a red cloth on his head. The general of his army has come too. Now the king has been watching, and he knows God has been taking care of Abraham. "We know God is with you," the king says. "Please promise to be a friend to me and my family." Abraham says, "All right." He and the king promise to be friends for a long time. Then the king and his general say good-bye and go back home. Now Abraham has a king for a friend. But, better than that, Abraham is God's friend.

QUESTIONS:

1. *Who has come to see Abraham?*
2. *What does the king want?*
3. *Why does the king want to be Abraham's friend?*
4. *What is better than being friends with a king?*

Genesis 21:22-24

ere is Abraham, talking to his best helper. Baby Isaac is grown up now, and Abraham says, "It is time for you to find a wife for my boy Isaac. I want you to go back to where I came from. Find my aunts and uncles and cousins. Bring back a girl from there to be Isaac's wife." "All right," the helper says. "But maybe she won't want to come so far. Shall I then take Isaac to her country?" But Abraham says, "No, no. God wants us to live here, and we will obey Him. He has promised this land to my children and their children. Isaac must live here." So the helper is taking ten camels. He will put many fine presents on their backs. And off he will go *plip plop* across the sand to find a wife for Isaac.

QUESTIONS:

1. *Who needs a wife?*
2. *Who is going to find a wife for Isaac?*
3. *Why does Abraham not want Isaac to go to a far-away place to live?*
4. *Who is being careful to obey God?*

Genesis 24:1-10

Here I am, Abraham's helper is thinking. *In Abraham's old country. But how shall I find the right wife for Isaac? I know. I will pray.* "O Lord," the helper prays, "help me find her. Here come the ladies to fill their water jars at the well. I shall ask one for a drink. If she says, 'Drink—and I will water your camels too,' let her be the right one." Now here comes Rebekah, carrying a jar of water. The helper will run to her and say, "Please—let me drink a little water from your jar." Rebekah will quickly say, "Drink—and I will water your camels too." Now Abraham's helper will know who is to be Isaac's wife. And he will thank God.

QUESTIONS:

1. Who asked God for help?
2. Who was polite?
3. Who thanked God?

Genesis 24:11-20

"Good-bye! Good-bye!" Rebekah is going on a long, long trip. She is going back with Abraham's helper to be Isaac's wife. Just this morning Rebekah's mother and brother asked her, "Will you go with this man?" And Rebekah said, "I will go." Now the camels are ready. Rebekah is riding a camel. Abraham's helper is riding a camel. More camels will carry other helpers. Rebekah's mother understands what God wants. Rebekah's brother understands what God wants. Rebekah understands what God wants. And they all say yes.

QUESTIONS:

1. *Where are the camels going?*
2. *Who is doing what God wants? Who else?*
3. *Do you think God is pleased?*

Genesis 24:55-61

Isaac and Rebekah waited a long time before there were any babies in their family. But now they have two boys—twin boys named Esau and Jacob. Here are Isaac and Rebekah at the door of their tent. They watch the boys play. The boys are different. Esau likes to be outside. He likes animals. Soon he will learn to hunt with a bow and arrow. He will be a good hunter. Jacob is a quiet boy. He likes to be inside. He stays close to home. Jacob and his mother talk while he plays near the tent. He will be a good cook. When the twins grow up they will look different. Their voices will sound different. Now, it is all right to be different in those ways. But something else will be different about these twins when they grow up. Jacob will believe God's words; Esau will not. And that is the biggest difference of all.

QUESTIONS:

1. What were the twins' names?
2. Which twin believed what God said?

Genesis 25:20-27

Isaac is an old man now. God has made him very rich. He has camels and sheep and a big garden and many men working for him. In this picture Isaac is watching his helpers dig a well. "Now we will have plenty of water," Isaac says. But, no, along come the king's men. "This is our water!" they say. Isaac does not want to fight about a well. He and his helpers dig a well in another place. "Now we will have plenty of water," Isaac says. But, no, along come the king's men. "This is our water!" they say. Isaac does not want to fight about a well. He and his helpers dig a well in another place. This time the king's men do not bother him. "At last the Lord has made room for us," Isaac says. "Now we shall have plenty of water." And they do.

QUESTIONS:

1. *Who gave Isaac camels and sheep and a big garden and many men to work for him?*
2. *Who is giving Isaac a place to live?*

Genesis 26:18-22

Isaac's boy Jacob is grown up now. Jacob is far away from home. Who is this man in the long coat? It is Jacob's Uncle Laban. A while ago Jacob stopped at this well. He said to some shepherds, "Do you know a man named Laban?" The shepherds said, "Yes, we know him. And here comes his girl Rachel with the sheep." Do you see Rachel? Quickly Jacob took the big stone off the top of the well. He gave Rachel's sheep a drink. Then he said, "I am your cousin Jacob. Your father, Laban, is my uncle." Rachel ran to get her father, and now he has come to meet Jacob. He is saying, "Come stay at my house!" Jacob is thankful to God for helping him find the right place.

QUESTIONS:

1. Who is far away from home?
2. Who helped Jacob find this place?
3. What is the name of the girl with the sheep?

Genesis 29:1-13

25

Jacob has lived with Uncle Laban for a long time. Now he is ready to go back home. He has wives and children and camels and donkeys and workers to help him. He has so much that Uncle Laban and his boys are thinking, *Jacob has too much.* That makes Jacob ready to listen when the Lord says to him, "Go back now to your country, where your father, Isaac, lives. And I will be with you." "Yes," say Rachel and Leah, Jacob's wives. "Do whatever God says to you." So here goes Jacob, obeying God. You can see just some of the many animals and people who are going with him.

QUESTIONS:

1. *Who told Jacob it was time to go back home?*
2. *What did God promise to do?*
3. *What did Rachel and Leah tell Jacob to do?*

Genesis 31:1-7; 14-18

Something very special is happening in this picture. Jacob and his family are back in their own country. God is talking to Jacob, and Jacob is listening. Jacob hears God say, "Your name is Jacob, but it won't be Jacob anymore. From now on your name will be *Israel*. You will have many children and grandchildren. Some of your family will be kings." Then God tells Jacob, "I gave this land to Abraham and Isaac. Now I will give it to you and your children." Then God will go away. But Jacob will remember what God has promised. Some day Jacob *will* have a very big family. And some of his family will be kings. For God always does just what He says He will do.

QUESTIONS:

1. *Who gave Jacob a new name?*
2. *What was it?*
3. *If God promises something, will He do it?*

Genesis 35:9-15

The boy wearing the beautiful coat is Joseph. His father, Jacob, gave it to him. His brothers are angry. They don't think Joseph should be the one to get special things. And soon there will be more trouble. Joseph is telling about a dream he had. "I dreamed we all were working in the wheat field," he says. "I saw my bunch of wheat stand up, and yours all bowed down to it." "What!" say Joseph's brothers. "Do you think you are going to be king over us?" And the brothers are angrier than before. But God gave Joseph that dream. God knows everything. He knows that someday Joseph *will* rule over his brothers—and other people too—just like a king.

QUESTIONS:

1. *Who has a beautiful coat?*
2. *Why are the brothers angry?*
3. *What makes more trouble?*
4. *What is Joseph going to do some day?*

Genesis 37:5-11

ere comes Joseph, wearing his fine coat. But look at his brothers. Such angry faces. What is happening? Well, not long ago their father, Jacob, said, "Joseph, your brothers are out with the sheep. Go see how they are and how the sheep are doing, and let me know." The brothers see him coming. "Here he comes," they say. "This one who dreams he will be king over us—let's kill him. Let's tell our father a wild animal ate him up." But don't you worry about Joseph. God will take care of Joseph. God has something special for Joseph to do.

QUESTIONS:

1. *What did father Jacob tell Joseph to do?*
2. *What are the brothers planning to do?*
3. *Why don't you need to worry about Joseph?*

Genesis 37:12-20

Poor Joseph. Look at him down in that deep hole. Some of his angry brothers wanted to kill him, but his oldest brother, Reuben, said no. So, instead, they took off Joseph's beautiful coat and threw him down into this pit. Joseph can't get out. Soon there will be more trouble. Some men will ride past on their camels. The brothers will pull Joseph out and sell him to the men! Then the men will take Joseph away. But don't worry. God will take care of Joseph. God has something special for Joseph to do.

QUESTIONS:

1. *How did Joseph get into that pit?*
2. *What will happen to him next?*
3. *Why don't you need to worry about Joseph?*
4. *Who has something special for Joseph to do?*

Genesis 37:23-28

C an this be Joseph? Yes, it is. How did he get
to this place? Those men on the camels did it.
They took Joseph to a far-away city. They sold him to
a soldier who wanted Joseph to work in his house.
God is helping Joseph to do good work. The
soldier—see him?—likes Joseph. He is letting Joseph
tell everybody in his house what to do. But soon there
will be trouble. The soldier's wife will tell lies about
Joseph. Then the soldier will become angry. He will
put Joseph in jail. But don't worry. God will take care
of Joseph. God has some special work for Joseph to
do.

QUESTIONS:

1. *What bad thing happened to Joseph in this
   story?*
2. *What good thing happened to Joseph?*
3. *What is God getting Joseph ready for?*

Genesis 39:1-6, 19-20

Joseph has a new job. Now he is working for the king. What has happened? The angry soldier put Joseph in jail, remember? One day God helped Joseph tell two men what their dreams meant. So when the king needed someone to tell him what *his* dream meant, they called Joseph. "Your dream," Joseph said, "means that bad times are coming. The gardens won't grow. Get ready now. Send a man to save up food all over the land." The king said, "God has made you wise. You do it." So here is Joseph, telling the king's people where to put the wheat. When the bad times come, and the gardens don't grow, there will be food for everybody. Joseph's new job is special. And God made him ready for it.

QUESTIONS:

1. *Who told the king what his dream meant?*
2. *Who told Joseph what the king's dream meant?*
3. *How is Joseph helping the king?*

Genesis 39:20; 40:7-8; 41:15-40

While Joseph is away, his father, Jacob, and his brothers are having trouble. Their gardens will not grow. Soon they will be hungry. At last Jacob says, "There is not enough to eat here. But I've heard we can buy wheat in Egypt. Go down to Egypt and buy some." Now we know that Joseph is in Egypt, working for the king. But his father and brothers don't know that. Joseph's ten brothers get their donkeys ready for the trip. Benjamin, Joseph's youngest brother, will not go along. Jacob says, "Benjamin must stay home. I'm afraid something might happen to him." So off the other brothers will go. They don't know that Joseph is in Egypt, but God knows. And God wants Joseph and his brothers to meet again.

QUESTIONS:

1. *What kind of trouble do Joseph's father and brothers have?*
2. *Who is going to Egypt to buy wheat?*
3. *Who stays at home?*
4. *Whom will the brothers see in Egypt?*

Genesis 42:1-5

33

Joseph's brothers have come to the land of Egypt. Can you guess who they are talking to? It's Joseph. But they don't know it's Joseph. They are saying, "Please let us buy some food." Joseph pretends he doesn't know them. He pretends to be angry. And he wonders where his little brother, Benjamin, is. "Take food for your families," Joseph says. "Then you must bring your youngest brother here." The brothers feel bad. They will talk to each other. They will say, "Oh, we are having trouble now because we were bad to Joseph long ago." They know they did wrong to sell Joseph. But they don't know that Joseph himself is listening to them talk. They will go now and bring back Benjamin.

QUESTIONS:

1. *Who is asking to buy food?*
2. *Who is Benjamin?*
3. *Who wants to see Benjamin?*
4. *Who remembers how bad they have been to Joseph?*

Genesis 42:8-23

Look at the parade. What are Joseph's brothers doing now? They brought Benjamin to Joseph. And Joseph told them he is their brother. Now they are going home to get their father, Jacob, and the rest of their family. All Joseph's family will come and live with him in Egypt. For Joseph is not angry with his brothers. He will say, "Don't worry. Yes, you meant to be bad to me. But God really sent me here to keep many people alive."

QUESTIONS:

1. *Who said, "Go get my father, and all of you may live here with me in Egypt"?*
2. *Who said, "Yes, you meant to be bad to me, but God sent me here to save the lives of many people"?*
3. *Who really sent Joseph to the land of Egypt?*
4. *Why?*

Genesis 45:4-11

35

Who is this angry man? He is the new king of Egypt. Joseph's family has lived in the king's country a long time. By now there are many mommies and daddies and grandmas and grandpas and aunts and uncles and brothers and sisters. The new king doesn't like that. He says to his soldiers, "These people are too many. Let's make them work hard and build some cities for us." Next he will say, "These people are still too many. When a baby boy is born you must throw him into the river." God's people are very tired and very unhappy. But don't worry. God knows what is happening, and He will send them a helper soon.

QUESTIONS:

1. *Why is the king angry?*
2. *What does the king say to do?*
3. *Who is going to send His people someone to help them?*

Exodus 1:7-14, 22

Here he is. Here is the helper God will send to His people. His name is Moses. He is still only a baby. The king says baby boys must be thrown into the river. But Moses' mother loves him. See what she is doing? She is putting baby Moses in a basket. Then she will hide the baby and the basket in the weeds of the river. No one should think to look for a baby *there*. Moses' big sister will stand near the river and watch him. Better than that, God will watch baby Moses. And Moses will grow up to be a leader for God's people.

QUESTIONS:

1. Why is Moses' mother going to hide him?
2. Why will she hide his basket in the weeds of the river instead of in the house?
3. Who will stand outside and watch the baby?
4. Who else will watch him?

Exodus 2:1-4

Now Moses is grown up. God has said to Moses, "Come. I will send you to the king. Tell him to let my people go out of his land." The king has been bad to God's people for a long time. He has made them work hard. Moses and his brother, Aaron, are brave. Here they go, up, up, up the steps to the king's house. It will be scary telling God's words to the king. The king won't want to listen. But Moses knows it is better to do what God says than to please a king.

QUESTIONS:

1. *Who told Moses to talk to the king?*
2. *Who told Moses what to say?*
3. *What is better than making a king happy?*

Exodus 3:7-10; 5:1-2

What are these people doing? They are God's people, and they are hurrying to get out of the king's country. The king's soldiers are chasing after them. When they saw the soldiers coming, the people were afraid. They said, "Oh! Here is water! We can't get across the water! The king's men will catch us!" But God always knows what to do, and He is strong enough to do it. See! He is holding back the water on this side and that side. And now the mommies and daddies and grandmas and grandpas and aunts and uncles and boys and girls aren't even getting their feet wet. Soon they will be safe, and the bad king will never hurt them again.

QUESTIONS:

1. *Why are God's people afraid?*
2. *What is God doing for them that nobody else can do?*
3. *Who is getting safely away from the king's soldiers?*

Exodus 14:9-10, 21-22

I s this where God made a path in the water for His people? No, not this time. Moses and the people have been walking for three days. They are thirsty. When they saw this water, they were glad. "Now we can have a nice cold drink," they said. But, *ugh!* The water isn't good, and everybody is so thirsty. But don't worry. God always knows what to do, and He is strong enough to do it. He shows Moses a special tree. Moses is throwing that tree into the water. Then the water will be good to drink, and everybody will have some.

QUESTIONS:

1. *What is wrong with the water?*
2. *What is Moses getting ready to do?*
3. *Who told Moses to do that?*
4. *What will happen to the water?*

Exodus 15:22-25

40

God's people are in trouble. But this man will help them. His name is Joshua. Joshua is a general. He knows how to lead soldiers. Some men have come to fight against God's people. Joshua has chosen some good soldiers to go with him. They will go to the bottom of this hill and fight the bad men who want to hurt them and their families. The bad people are strong. But God will make Joshua and his soldiers stronger, and they will win the battle.

QUESTIONS:

1. What is the general's name?
2. What is Joshua getting ready to do?
3. Who will make Joshua strong?

Deuteronomy 25:17-18; Exodus 17:8-10, 13

See Moses walking up the big hill. All the people are far, far below. They watch him go up. They see smoke and fire on the top of the mountain. They hear thunder and the sound of a trumpet blowing. They feel the mountain shaking. The people are afraid. Moses is afraid too. But he keeps on walking. God will come down and talk with Moses at the top of the hill. God will give Moses some good rules for the people. God's rules are always good. If God's people will do what He says, they will be happy.

QUESTIONS:

1. Where is Moses going?
2. Who wants to talk to him up there?
3. What will make God's people happy?

Exodus 19:17-20; 24:3

ere is Moses at the top of the mountain. Moses is listening, listening, because God is talking to him out of that cloud. God is telling Moses the good things He wants His people to do. He is saying, "I will send an angel with you. He will keep you and the people safe. He will go with you to the special land I have made ready for you." Then God says, "Be sure to do what He says, for I am sending Him." Now Moses will go down the mountain. He will tell the people what God said, and all the people will say, "Yes. All the words the Lord has spoken, we will do."

QUESTIONS:

1. Is Moses talking or listening?
2. Whom does God promise to send with Moses and the people?
3. Where will the angel take them?'
4. What will God's people say they will do?

Exodus 20:21-23; 24:3

43

God's people are taking a long trip. They are going to the beautiful new land God has made for them. At night they sleep in these tents. In the morning they get up and look at that special cloud. God has put that cloud there. If the cloud starts to move, they fold up their tents and go with it. If the cloud stays where it is, the people stay too. God has put the cloud there to show His people when to go and where to go and when to stay. God knows the way to the good new land. He will show His people how to get there.

QUESTIONS:

1. *Why are the people looking at the special cloud?*
2. *If the people go with the cloud, where will it take them?*
3. *Who put the cloud there?*

Numbers 9:15-23

44

"Here they come! Here they come!" God's people can hardly wait. God is giving them a new living place. Caleb and Joshua and some other men went to look at it. Now they are coming back. They are carrying something. Soon all these people will crowd around them, trying to see. "What's our new land like? Oh, what nice fruit you found! It *must* be a good place to live. Did you see any people? What's that? Giants! You saw giants?" Just thinking about giants will make everybody afraid. Quickly Caleb and Joshua will say, "Don't worry. The Lord is with us. He will help us fight the giants." But God's people will say no. No, they won't believe God is stronger than giants. No, they won't believe He can take care of them. No, they won't go into their new land. No. No. No. No. No.

QUESTIONS:

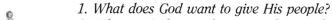

1. *What does God want to give His people?*
2. *Why won't the people go into the new land?*
3. *Is God stronger than giants?*

Numbers 13:25-33; 14:6-10

Something about this picture is sad. God's people have just said no to Him. "No, we won't go into that new country. Giants live there. They will kill us. They will take away our boys and girls." The people cried and fussed. Now God is sending them back into the wild and dry place they've just come from. Now they won't get into the beautiful country—ever. Now they will have to walk around and around for a long time. What bad news—all because they wouldn't obey. Now there's some good news, too. Caleb and Joshua want to obey. God says that some day Caleb and Joshua will get into the beautiful land. And the grown-up boys and girls will go in. But isn't it sad that the mommies and the daddies wouldn't do what God said?

QUESTIONS:

1. *Where are all the people going now?*
2. *Why are they going away?*
3. *What is the happy part of this story?*

Numbers 14:26-31

W alking. Walking. God's people are walking. They did not believe God would take care of them in their beautiful new country. So now they are having to walk here and there in a big, dry, rocky place. That is bad news. The good news is that the Lord God is taking care of them even here. When they are hungry, He gives them special food from heaven. One day when they are thirsty He will make water come out of a big rock for them. They will walk a long time, but their coats won't wear out. Their feet will stay well and strong. The people don't deserve to have God be so good to them. But that's the way God is. He likes to be kind.

QUESTIONS:

1. *Where are the people?*
2. *Who feeds them?*
3. *Who keeps their clothes from getting holes?*
4. *Why does God do these good things?*

Deuteronomy 8:2-4, 15-16

Soldier Joshua is the leader of God's people now. He is the one with the stripes on his head cover. God's people are in their new country. God has told Joshua and his soldiers to fight against the bad people who live there. He doesn't want His people to live with people who won't listen to God. But what is this? Joshua is talking to one of those men. (Be careful, Joshua! He's trying to fool you!) The man and his friends (see them?) are lying to Joshua. "You don't want to fight against us," they say. "We don't even live here. We have come from far away. See our clothes, how old they are. See the bread from our lunch, how old and dry it is. Do say you will be our friends." (Be careful, Joshua! Ask God what to do!) But Joshua doesn't ask God what to do. He just says, "All right." What a big mistake. When we don't do what God says, there is always trouble.

QUESTIONS:

1. *Who is the new leader of God's people?*
2. *Why did God tell Joshua to fight against the bad people?*
3. *What did Joshua forget to do?*

Joshua 9:3-16

48

Remember Joshua's friend Caleb? All his life Caleb has tried to do what God wants. Remember when Caleb and Joshua said to everybody, "Come! God wants us to go into the new land He has given us. He will help us fight the giants!" But no one would listen. See how old Caleb is now. But he still tries to do what God wants. Caleb is saying to Joshua, "See? Here is the land Moses said I could have. God has let me live until now. I am old, but I am strong. If the Lord is with me I shall drive the giants out." Now Caleb knows God is with him. He *will* chase out the giants. And their city will belong to him. God likes to help the people who try to please Him.

QUESTIONS:

1. *Who is Joshua's friend?*
2. *Who will help Caleb chase away the giants?*
3. *What people does God like to help?*

Joshua 14:6-14

ere come some ladies to talk with Joshua. How many are there? What do you suppose they want? The ladies are sisters, and they need Joshua's help. All the sisters' boy cousins have been given land to live on. "But we don't have any boys in our family," they say. "God told Moses to be sure to give us land just like our boy cousins." The sisters don't need to worry. Joshua will do just what God has said. He will give each one of them a place to live in the beautiful new country.

QUESTIONS:

1. *Who don't have a place to live yet?*
2. *Does God care about girls as well as boys?*
3. *How do you know?*

Joshua 17:3-4

Joshua is talking to all the leaders today. He is standing where everybody can see him, and all the men are listening. "Remember what the Lord has done for you," he says. "He helped you get away from the bad king. He led you to this good land. He helped your soldiers fight. He gave you cities to live in. He gave you food to eat. So obey God. Do what pleases Him." Then, while everybody is still listening, Joshua says, "I don't know what you are going to do, but my family and I—*we* will do what God says." And all the people say, "We will obey Him too."

QUESTIONS:

1. *Who is talking to the leaders?*
2. *Why are all the men standing there?*
3. *What does Joshua want them to do?*

Joshua 24:1-16

51

These men don't look like soldiers, but that is what they are. Their leader is Gideon here. That is a kind of horn he is holding. That is a burning stick in his other hand. Well, very many people called Midianites have come. They want to steal sheep and cows and donkeys. God has shown Gideon what to do. It is night, and all the Midianites are asleep in their camping place. Gideon and his men are going to cover up their fiery lights with water jars. They will make a big circle around the sleeping army. Then—*smash*—they will break the jars and hold the lights high. They will shout in loud voices and blow their horns. Such a noise! The Midianites will wake up. They will start to fight each other, and all the army will run away.

QUESTIONS:

1. *Why did the Midianite people come?*
2. *Who told Gideon what to do?*
3. *Does God know how to help His people when they need help?*

Judges 7:16-22

52

This old man is Samuel. He is praying for God's people. See all the people standing there. They are listening while he prays. Samuel has loved God for a long time. He loves people too. Samuel saw when the people were not obeying God. Samuel said, "Come back to God. Obey Him. Then God will save you from the bad Philistine people." The people listened. They threw away the stone things they had been praying to. They tried to please God. Samuel told them all to come to this place, and he would pray for them. When the Philistine people heard about it, they got ready to fight. Everyone is afraid. But Samuel is praying, and the Lord is listening. Soon God will make the thunder rumble very loud. The Philistine soldiers won't know what to do. They will start to run. God's people will chase them, and the Philistines won't come back for a long time.

QUESTIONS:

1. What is the old man's name?
2. What is he doing?
3. How do you know God listened to Samuel's prayer?

1 Samuel 7:3-13

53

See how old Samuel is now. The leaders think he is too old to tell them what to do anymore. A while ago they told Samuel, "You are old now. Give us a king. Everybody else has a king." That didn't seem right to Samuel, and he talked to the Lord about it. "The people don't want me to tell them what to do anymore." The Lord said, "Samuel, I am the one they don't want. They don't want Me to be their king. Tell them how much trouble they will have if they get a king." In this picture Samuel is telling them that the king will take their boys and girls to work for him. He will take their gardens. He will take their money. He will take their donkeys. But the men say, "No, we still want a king." God will let them have a king, but some day they will be sorry.

QUESTIONS:

1. *Why are the men talking to Samuel?*
2. *Do the people want Samuel to be their king?*
3. *Whom else don't they want?*

1 Samuel 8:4-22

This should be a happy picture. Samuel is showing the people their new king. The people are pleased. Now they have a king like all the other people. But this is not a happy picture. It is a sad picture. God Himself is the people's king. But they want someone they can see. They won't listen to Samuel. They don't want what God wants. They just want what they want. When the people see that the new king, Saul, is tall and strong and fine looking, they cheer with loud voices. They think, *Now we have what we want.*

QUESTIONS:

1. *What is the name of the new king?*
2. *Is Samuel pleased that Saul is king?*
3. *Why do the people think Saul will be a good king?*

1 Samuel 10:17-24

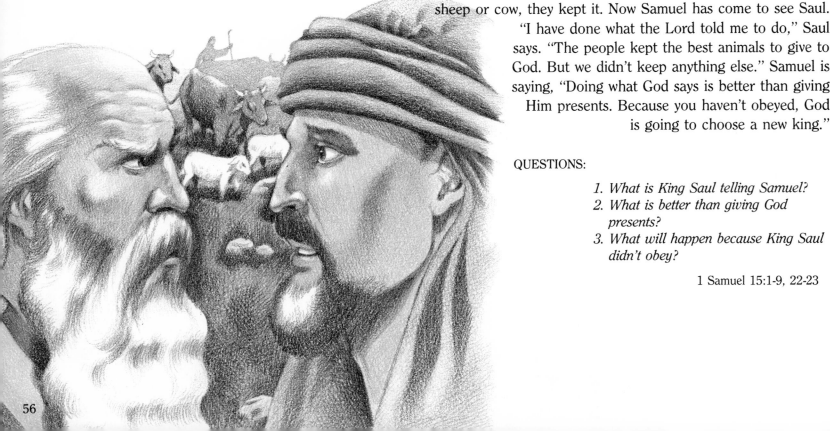

Why does Samuel look so unhappy? I'll tell you why. Some people, called Amalek, tried to hurt God's people. So the Lord sent King Saul to fight against them. Their city was so bad that Saul wasn't to save alive even the animals in it. Out went King Saul's soldiers. They fought against the city. They chased the people of Amalek a long, long way. But whenever they saw a good sheep or cow, they kept it. Now Samuel has come to see Saul.

"I have done what the Lord told me to do," Saul says. "The people kept the best animals to give to God. But we didn't keep anything else." Samuel is saying, "Doing what God says is better than giving Him presents. Because you haven't obeyed, God is going to choose a new king."

QUESTIONS:

1. *What is King Saul telling Samuel?*
2. *What is better than giving God presents?*
3. *What will happen because King Saul didn't obey?*

1 Samuel 15:1-9, 22-23

ne day the Lord sent Samuel to Bethlehem. (Jesus was not a baby there yet.) The Lord said, "I want one of Jesse's boys to be the next king." But He did not tell Samuel which one. At Jesse's house, Samuel saw the oldest boy. He was big and fine looking. Samuel thought, *This must be the next king*. But the Lord said, "No, not this one. Never mind his looks. People look on the *outside* of a man, but God sees what kind of person he is *inside*." Samuel looked at each of Jesse's boys. But God said no each time. Now they are bringing David. He is a big boy but not very old yet. He was out taking care of the sheep. He doesn't look like a king. But the Lord is saying to Samuel, "This is the one. Make him the next king."

QUESTIONS:

1. *Why did Samuel go to Bethlehem?*
2. *Who was taking care of the sheep?*
3. *Who could look inside David and know he would be a good king?*

1 Samuel 16:1-12

57

The man in the green coat is David. David is not king yet. Every day he works for King Saul. And Saul knows David will be king someday. Saul wants to kill David. But God has given David a friend in King Saul's house. It is Jonathan, the king's big boy, and here he is. Jonathan loves David very much. He loves the Lord too. Jonathan helps David. It is not safe for David to be in the king's house anymore. So David and Jonathan are talking out in the field. Jonathan is saying, "You must go away to be safe, but we shall always be friends."

QUESTIONS:

1. Whom did God give David as a friend?
2. Why must David go away?
3. Why does King Saul want to hurt David?

1 Samuel 20:35-42

Why are these men hurrying down the big hill? They are David and his men, and they are hurrying to get away. King Saul and his soldiers are coming up the other side of the hill. They want to kill David. What can David do? Don't worry. God knows how to help. A man will run to King Saul saying, "Quick! Come back home! We need you and the army! The Philistine people have come to fight us!" King Saul will stop chasing David. He will decide to go home. And David and his men will be safe.

QUESTIONS:

1. *Why are the men in such a hurry?*
2. *Who knows how to help David?*
3. *How does He help?*

1 Samuel 23:24-28

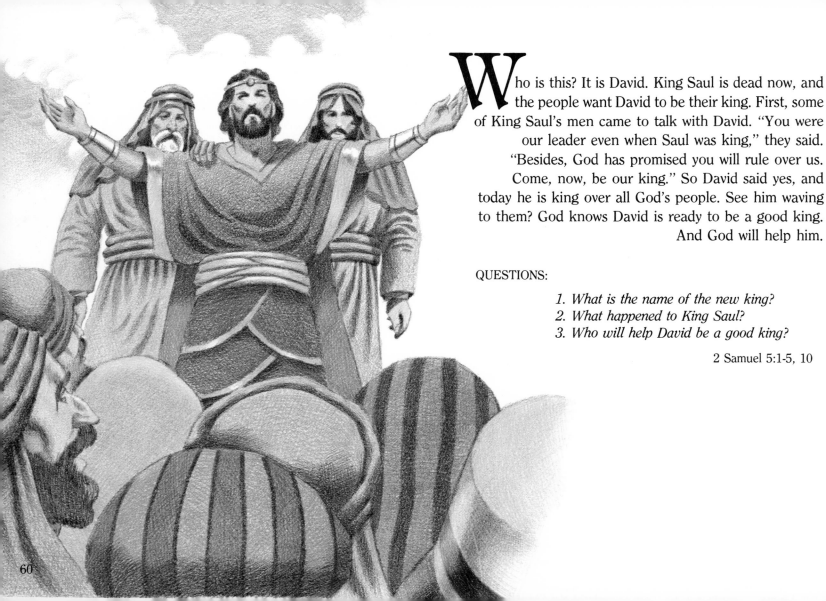

Who is this? It is David. King Saul is dead now, and the people want David to be their king. First, some of King Saul's men came to talk with David. "You were our leader even when Saul was king," they said. "Besides, God has promised you will rule over us. Come, now, be our king." So David said yes, and today he is king over all God's people. See him waving to them? God knows David is ready to be a good king. And God will help him.

QUESTIONS:

1. *What is the name of the new king?*
2. *What happened to King Saul?*
3. *Who will help David be a good king?*

2 Samuel 5:1-5, 10

60

Who is this poor man? We haven't seen him before, but he is Jonathan's grown-up boy, Mephibosheth. After David was king for a while, he said to himself, "Jonathan was a good friend to me. I loved him. I wonder if he has any family left. I'd like to be good to someone in Jonathan's family because I loved Jonathan so much." Somebody told King David, "Jonathan has one boy left. He lives in such and such a place. But he can't walk well. Both his feet are sick." David didn't care about that. He sent for Mephibosheth. Now David is telling Mephibosheth not to be afraid. He will give Mephibosheth some land. He will let Mephibosheth eat at the king's table just like the king's own boys.

QUESTIONS:

1. *What is the name of Jonathan's big boy?*
2. *What is wrong with Mephibosheth?*
3. *Why will David be good to Mephibosheth?*

2 Samuel 9:1-7

See the fine house David lives in now. He is the king, and his house is made of beautiful wood. David likes his house. But David has been thinking. He says to his friend Nathan, "Why should I live in a beautiful house like this when there is no special building for God? That does not seem right." David thinks he would like to build a fine temple-church for God. But that's not what God is thinking. David is not to build the temple-church. God says that David's boy Solomon will build it someday. Now David knows God always does what is right. So David says, "All right. Then I'll get things ready for Solomon to build God's house." And he will.

QUESTIONS:

1. *Who is the man sitting in the big chair?*
2. *What does David want to do?*
3. *Who will build God's temple-church?*
4. *What will David do to help?*

2 Samuel 7:1-2; 1 Chronicles 22:5-10

King David is old now. He knows he won't be king much longer. David is showing his grown-up boy Solomon some of the stone and wood he has made ready for building the temple-church. "You are to build God's temple," David said. "I wanted to, but God said no. He wants you to do it when you are king." He tells Solomon about the gold and silver that he has saved. David says, "Solomon, you have many fine workers to help you. Be strong and brave. Build the Lord's temple-church. And be careful to do what God says."

QUESTIONS:

1. Who is going to build the temple church?
2. How did King David help Solomon?
3. What should Solomon be careful to do?

1 Chronicles 22:6-16

What a happy day! Here comes Solomon, the new king, riding on David's own mule. David is too old to be king now. He told his friends to make Solomon king. So all the people are shouting. Some start to make music with horns. The noise is so loud that the earth shakes. People far away can hear it. The whole city is happy from one end to the other. And what is God doing? God is keeping His promise. Long ago He promised David that Solomon would be the next king. And he is. God always does just what He says He will do.

QUESTIONS:

1. *Who is the new king?*
2. *Who is his daddy?*
3. *How do you know the people are happy?*

1 Kings 1:32-40

What is King Solomon doing? It is night time. Solomon is sleeping, and he is having a dream. In his dream God comes and talks to Solomon. God says, "Ask Me for something. What do you want Me to give you?" Do you think Solomon will ask for a horse? Will he ask for bags of gold? Maybe he will ask to live a long time. No, Solomon doesn't ask for any of those things. Solomon, in his dream, says, "Oh, You have made me king, and I don't know how to be king. Please make me wise so that I'll be a good king over all Your people." The Lord is pleased to hear Solomon say that. And do you know what? The Lord will make Solomon the wisest man in the world.

QUESTIONS:

1. *Who talked to King Solomon in his dream?*
2. *What did the Lord tell Solomon to do?*
3. *What did Solomon ask for?*
4. *Will God make him wise?*

1 Kings 3:5-15

H ere is King Solomon again. This time he is sitting in his beautiful chair. And who are all these men? They have come from far, far away just to hear King Solomon talk. For Solomon knows many things. He talks about trees and bushes and animals and birds and fish and crawling things. When people need to know what is right, they come to Solomon, and he tells them. King Solomon is the wisest man in the world. Who has made him that way? It's God who did it. And even Solomon is not as wise as God.

QUESTIONS:

1. *Who is the king?*
2. *Why do people come to hear him talk?*
3. *Who is wiser than Solomon?*

1 Kings 4:29-34

Look at who is coming to visit King Solomon today. It is the Queen of Sheba. She has come from a far, far-away land. The queen heard about wise King Solomon in her country. Now she is coming to ask him some questions. She is bringing presents too—gold and other special things. Soon the queen will see Solomon's beautiful house. She will see his helpers and his food. She will ask him questions, and he will answer them all. She will say, "I heard how wise you are. But you are even wiser and richer than they told me." I wonder what questions the queen will ask Solomon. Do you suppose she will ask him about the Lord God?

QUESTIONS:

1. *Whose camels are these?*
2. *Where is the queen going?*
3. *Will Solomon know the answers to her questions?*

1 Kings 10:1-11

See the big boy in the yellow coat. This is Rehoboam. He is the new king over God's people. But I'm sorry to tell you he will not be a good king. You see, Rehoboam will not listen. A while ago the people came and said to him, "Please don't make us work so hard." But Rehoboam would not listen. These old men are saying, "Be good to the people." But Rehoboam will not listen. He will do what his friends say. He won't ask God to make him wise, either. Rehoboam will be a very foolish king.

QUESTIONS:

1. What is the new king's name?
2. What are the old men telling Rehoboam?
3. Will Rehoboam listen to them?
4. Who is going to be a very foolish king?

1 Kings 12:1-8

This man is King Abijah. But what is he doing up there? Another king and his big army have come to fight. Abijah told his own men to wait. Then he climbed up high. Now the other soldiers can see him. They can hear him. Abijah is safe up there. "Listen!" he says. "You are making a mistake. God is with us. Don't fight against us. You will be fighting against God. You will never win." The other army hears him, but they will not listen. They will start to fight. Quickly King Abijah and his men will say, "Lord, help us!" And God will help. The other army will run away.

QUESTIONS:

1. Why did Abijah climb the high hill?
2. Can the other soldiers hear him?
3. Whom will Abijah's men ask for help?
4. Will God hear their prayer?

2 Chronicles 13:1-12, 18

Now it is Asa's turn to be king. Asa is a wise king. He loves the Lord God. He does what God says. He tells the people to obey God too. But even kings who try to please the Lord have trouble sometimes. One day Asa hears that an army is coming to fight—a big army. Asa's own little army is not strong enough to win. But Asa knows Someone who is strong. Here is Asa with his soldiers, and Asa is praying, "Lord, there is nobody to help us but You. So help us, Lord our God. We are Your people." And God will do what King Asa asks. When the fighting starts, the big army will run away and not come back.

QUESTIONS:

1. *Now whose turn is it to be king?*
2. *Why do Asa and his soldiers need help?*
3. *Who is strong enough to make the big army run away?*

2 Chronicles 14:1-4, 9-12

This story is about God's man Elijah. It hadn't rained for a long time. The gardens wouldn't grow. People didn't have enough to eat. One day Elijah met this lady. "Please," he said, "let me have a drink of water. And a piece of bread too." The lady said, "Oh, my. All I have is a tiny bit of cooking flour and oil. When that's gone, my boy and I won't have anything to eat." But Elijah said, "Don't worry. Make me a little roll first. Then make one for you and your boy. God says you will have enough flour and oil to cook with until the gardens grow again." Well, the lady knows God will do what He says. Here she is giving Elijah a nice roll. Now she will make some for herself and her boy. And God will not let the flour bowl or the oil jar get empty.

QUESTIONS:

1. Why didn't the people have enough to eat?
2. What is happening in the picture?
3. What did God say about the lady's flour bowl and oil jar?

1 Kings 17:7-16

71

W hy is God's man Elijah running so fast? He is
trying to get away from the bad queen. She
wants to kill him. But don't worry. God won't let that
happen. Soon Elijah will stop to rest. God will tell an
angel to bring him some nice bread to eat and some
water to drink. Then Elijah will keep on going until he
is far, far away from the queen. But Elijah won't be far,
far away from God. The Lord God will be in that
place. He is everywhere. He will talk to Elijah. He will
give Elijah some new work to do.

QUESTIONS:

1. *Why is Elijah running away?*
2. *Whom does God send to help Elijah?*
3. *Who is with us even when we are in
   far-away places?*

1 Kings 19:1-16

lijah is old now. Soon he will not be able to travel around. Somebody else will have to tell the people what God wants them to do. God knows that. He has somebody ready to take Elijah's place. So one day the Lord said to Elijah, "Go find a man called Elisha. He lives in such and such a place. He will tell My words to the people when you are gone." In the picture Elijah has just found Elisha. He will walk close and put his coat on Elisha. Elisha will know what that means. He is to go with the old man and help him. Elisha will say good-bye to his mommy and daddy. Then he will go with Elijah and learn how to be God's man.

QUESTIONS:

1. *Why did someone have to take Elijah's place?*
2. *Did God know who was best to take Elijah's place?*
3. *Does God know right now what work you should do when you grow up?*

1 Kings 19:15-21

Here is Micaiah, talking with two kings. Just a while ago a man came to his house. "Micaiah," he said, "King Ahab wants you. He is asking if he should take the army and go out to fight. Everybody is saying yes. You say yes too." But God made Micaiah strong inside. He said, "I'll say only what the Lord tells me to say." Now bad King Ahab is asking, "Micaiah, shall we take the army and go out to fight?" Micaiah knows everybody else has said yes. But Micaiah knows what God wants, and God makes Micaiah strong inside. Micaiah says no. He tells the king what will happen. Many soldiers will be hurt. King Ahab himself will be killed. Well, when King Ahab hears that he gets very angry. He will tell his men to lock up Micaiah. But Micaiah knows he said what God told him to say, and Micaiah is not sorry.

QUESTIONS:

1. *Who wanted to talk to Micaiah?*
2. *What does the king want Micaiah to tell him?*
3. *Who makes Micaiah strong inside?*

1 Kings 22:10, 14, 17, 26-28

A king has many things to do. King Jehoshaphat is a good king, but he has too many things to do all by himself. Many times God's people need someone to tell them what they should do. If Jehoshaphat talks to everybody, he will not have time to eat or sleep. So here is the king, choosing some helpers. He will put helpers in every city. They will be there when the people need to ask anything. Jehoshaphat is saying, "Be careful. You will be working for God. He will be with you. When people come to you with their troubles, be strong inside. Help them by telling them what is right."

QUESTIONS:

1. *Why does the king need helpers?*
2. *Where will the helpers live?*
3. *Whom will the helpers really be working for?*

2 Chronicles 19:4-11

King Jehoshaphat is afraid. The people are afraid too. Many soldiers are coming to fight them. The king is praying, while the people listen. He is saying, "Lord, You are God. You are the strong one. We can't do anything to help ourselves against all these soldiers. We are waiting for You to help us." Just then one of God's men calls out, "Listen! God says don't be afraid. You won't even need to fight tomorrow. The Lord is with you!" Jehoshaphat and the people believe God. In the morning special singers will walk in front of Jehoshaphat's men. They will sing and thank the Lord. The enemy soldiers will start to fight each other. They won't fight the king at all. And King Jehoshaphat and his people will sing and make music all the way home.

QUESTIONS:

1. *Why is the king afraid?*
2. *What is he doing in the picture?*
3. *Who is stronger than a big army?*

2 Chronicles 20:2-6, 12-18, 27-28

See the man with the green on his coat. This is Gehazi. He works for God's man Elisha. Gehazi isn't happy. He wants more things than he has. One day a sick soldier came to see Elisha. God made the soldier well. He was so happy he tried to give Elisha some clothes and silver money. Elisha said no, but Gehazi was listening. *I would like some presents,* he thought. So when the soldier left in his special wagon, Gehazi ran after him. And here he is, telling lies. "Elisha sent me." That is a lie. "Two men have just come to visit." That is a lie. "Elisha wants me to ask you for money and clothes for them." That is a lie, too. The soldier doesn't know Gehazi is lying. But God knows. He wants Gehazi to say what is right. Gehazi thinks he will wear the clothes and spend the money. But soon Gehazi will be too sick to be happy with the presents he lied to get.

QUESTIONS:

 1. *Did Elisha want the money and clothes?*
 2. *Who did want them?*
 3. *What did Gehazi do to get the presents?*
 4. *Will he be happy with them?*

2 Kings 5:14-16, 20-27

The baby boy is named Joash. His aunt is holding him. She loves him very much. His grandmother is the queen, but she is a bad queen. She has killed baby Joash's big brothers so that she can be queen all by herself. God will not let Joash be killed. He helped Aunt Jehosheba think fast. She hid baby Joash, and nobody saw her do it. Now she has taken him to the temple-church. Her husband works there. See him? Aunt Jehosheba will take care of baby Joash. He will sleep in the temple-church. He will play there. The bad queen won't find Joash. And he will be the next king.

QUESTIONS:

1. What is the baby's name?
2. Who is holding him?
3. Does the bad queen know where he is?

2 Chronicles 22:10-12; 23:11

Remember Joash, the baby who lived in the temple-church? He grew up to be a good king. One day he looked around and said, "Oh, my. People have not been taking care of God's temple. We must make it look nice again." So Joash took a big box and made a hole in the top. Now all the people who want God's temple to look nice again are dropping money into the box. Soon there will be enough money to pay the wood workers and the stone workers and the metal workers to make the temple-church beautiful again. God is helping His people remember that pleasing Him is the most important thing they can do.

QUESTIONS:

1. *Where are the people going?*
2. *What is that box for?*
3. *What will the money be used for?*
4. *Will God be pleased?*

2 Chronicles 24:1-12

S ometimes God's people had good kings. Sometimes they had bad kings. Here is good King Jotham. He is looking at some building his men are doing. Jotham thinks about the Lord and tries hard to do what is right. Jotham likes to build things. He told his men to build this wall. See how beautiful it is? He will build gates and cities and towers and forts. He is a good king. But Jotham is not a good king because he is a builder. He is a good king because he is careful to do the things the Lord wants him to do.

QUESTIONS:

1. *What did King Jotham like to do?*
2. *Was Jotham a good king or a bad king?*
3. *What made him a good king?*

2 Chronicles 27:1-6

Let me tell you a sad story. See the man in the red coat? He started off as a good king, but now he has made a big mistake. God has let Uzziah be king for a long time. At first he kept thinking of what God said good kings should do. And the Lord helped him. His soldiers chased off anybody who came to fight against them. Other people brought him money. He built towers. He made his army strong. But then Uzziah began to think what a fine king he was. "I can do anything I want to," he said one day. "I will go into the temple-church and do what God's workers do there." But the temple workers say, "No, Uzziah. God says no." They are hurrying Uzziah out. He won't be able to go into the temple again. Uzziah's big mistake was to start thinking how fine he was.

QUESTIONS:

1. Who helped Uzziah be a strong king?
2. What is happening in this picture?
3. What was Uzziah's big mistake?

2 Chronicles 26:3-20

What is this? King Ahaz is praying, but he is not asking the Lord for help. He is praying to an idol. This king has never paid attention to God's Book. When he wants to pray to an idol, he does. When he wants to kill some of his babies, he does. When he wants to shut up the temple-church so people can't get in, he does. The saddest thing is that King Ahaz makes his people want to pray to idols too. But the Lord knows what to do. He will let big trouble come to Ahaz and his people. And that is good, because trouble sometimes helps people remember God.

QUESTIONS:

1. What is King Ahaz doing?
2. Does he like to read God's Book?
3. What will happen to the king and his people?

2 Chronicles 28:1-5, 22-25

King Hezekiah is standing in front of the big temple-church. He hasn't been king very long. But Hezekiah loves the Lord God very much. He wants to do what God says. Right away he told his helpers to open the doors of the temple-church. Now people can get in to pray. In this picture Hezekiah is talking to his helpers. He says, "Let us clean up God's temple. Our fathers and grandfathers forgot about pleasing God. So we have had many troubles. Let us now do what God says." The helpers will work hard. They will clean every part of the temple-church. Then everybody will come together to make music and pray and sing words from the Bible. What a happy day!

QUESTIONS:

1. Who said, "Open the temple-church doors"?
2. Who will go in to pray?
3. What will the king's helpers do next?

2 Chronicles 29

his is a room in King Hezekiah's beautiful house. God has made Hezekiah very rich. He has gold and silver and sparkly stones and cows and sheep and many cities. But today Hezekiah is not thinking about what God has done. He is being foolish. He is just thinking about showing off all his nice things. These men have come from a far-away place. It makes Hezekiah feel good to have so many nice things to show them. I'm afraid Hezekiah has grown proud, and that is bad news. These men will go back and tell their king what Hezekiah has. Then soldiers will come to take the beautiful things away.

QUESTIONS:

1. *What is happening in the picture?*
2. *Who gave Hezekiah his beautiful things?*
3. *Who will take them away?*

2 Chronicles 32:27-29; 2 Kings 20:12-17

How sad Manesseh looks. He used to be king over God's people. But now see the chains on his hands? What has happened? When Manasseh was king, he wouldn't listen to God. He prayed to idols. He made his people want to pray to idols too. He killed some of his babies. He even put an idol in the temple-church. The Lord gave him a chance to do right. But Manasseh wouldn't listen. So one day some soldiers came. They caught Manasseh and locked him up far away from home. The good part is that when he was in trouble, Manasseh changed his mind. "I have been wrong," he is saying to God. "I am sorry." God will hear him. God will forgive him. And when Manasseh gets to be king again, he will take that idol out of the temple-church. He will tell the people, "Listen to the Lord God. Do what He says."

QUESTIONS:

1. What is this man doing?
2. Why is he having so much trouble?
3. What will he do when he is king again?

2 Chronicles 33:1-16

Josiah is only eight years old, but it is his turn to be king. The Lord knows even now that Josiah will be a good leader. Josiah is only eight years old. But the Lord knows Josiah will try to please Him. Josiah is only eight years old. But the Lord knows that some day Josiah will break down those ugly things people are praying to. Josiah is only eight years old. But the Lord knows that some day Josiah will say, "The temple-church needs to be fixed up again. Tell the workers to do it." Josiah is only eight years old. But the Lord knows that some day people will find God's Book in the temple-church. And Josiah will want to do what God's Book says.

QUESTIONS:

1. How old is this new king?
2. Who knows all about him?
3. Will Josiah try to please the Lord?

2 Kings 22:1-13

Why does this old man look so surprised? Hilkiah works in God's temple-church, and he has just found something very special. You see, nobody has been taking care of God's temple-church for a long time. Some things are dirty. Some things are broken. And some things are lost. Nobody knew where God's Book was. No one had opened it and read to the people for a long time. One day King Josiah said, "Come, let's give the wood workers and the stone workers some money. Let them fix up the temple-church so that it looks good again." And while they were working, Hilkiah saw this rolled-up book. He looked. Then he looked again. "It's God's Book!" said Hilkiah. "We have found it! We must tell the king." And that is what they did.

QUESTIONS:

    1. What was lost?
    2. Where was it lost?
    3. Who found it?

                2 Chronicles 34:1, 8-16

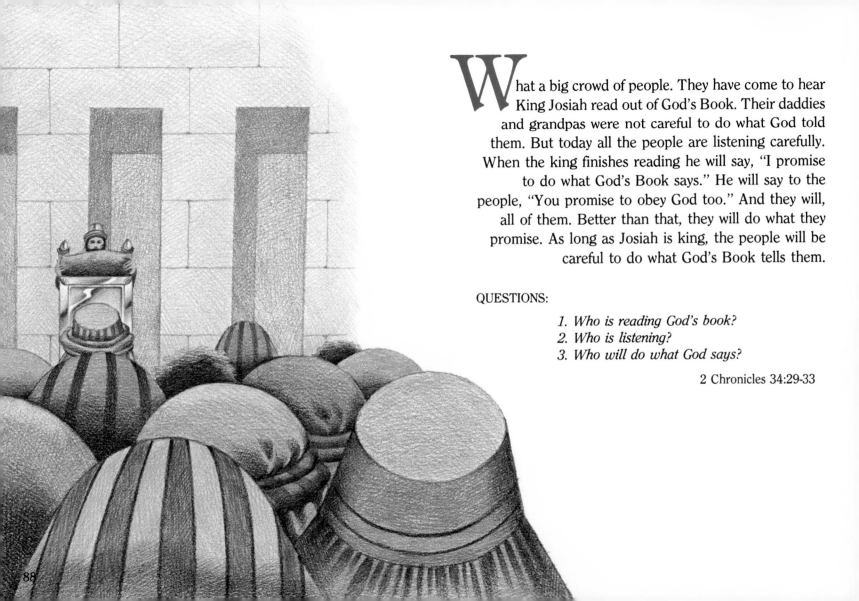

What a big crowd of people. They have come to hear King Josiah read out of God's Book. Their daddies and grandpas were not careful to do what God told them. But today all the people are listening carefully. When the king finishes reading he will say, "I promise to do what God's Book says." He will say to the people, "You promise to obey God too." And they will, all of them. Better than that, they will do what they promise. As long as Josiah is king, the people will be careful to do what God's Book tells them.

QUESTIONS:

1. *Who is reading God's book?*
2. *Who is listening?*
3. *Who will do what God says?*

2 Chronicles 34:29-33

Nehemiah is far, far away from home. He works for the king. He has all the food he needs. He has all the clothes he needs. But Nehemiah is sad. He has just heard bad news about the city he used to live in. Its gates have been burned. Its walls are broken down. Nehemiah is telling the king and queen. The king says, "What would you like me to do for you?" Quickly Nehemiah prays. The king can't hear him. But God can hear. Nehemiah will ask the king to let him go and build up the broken-down walls. And the king will say yes.

QUESTIONS:

1. Why is Nehemiah sad?
2. What will the king ask Nehemiah?
3. What does Nehemiah do before he tells the king?

Nehemiah 2:1-6

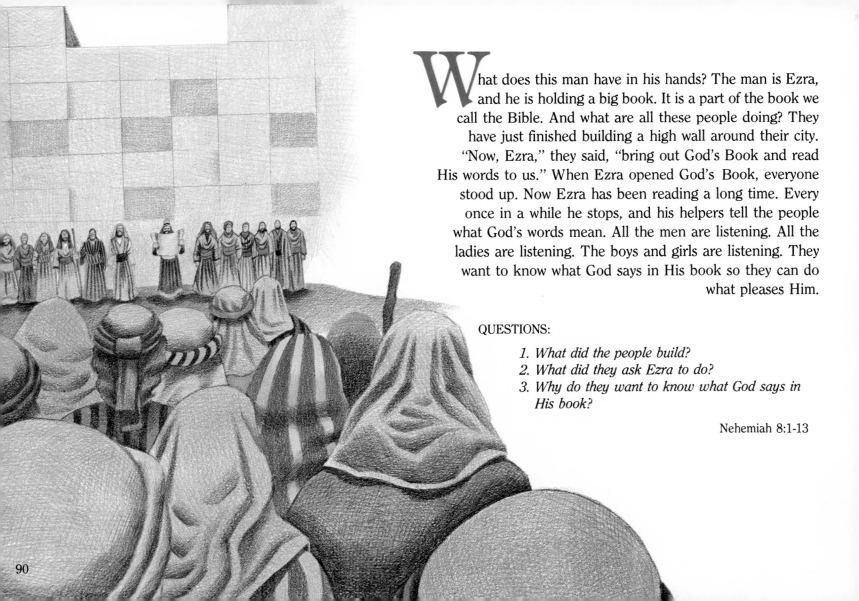

hat does this man have in his hands? The man is Ezra, and he is holding a big book. It is a part of the book we call the Bible. And what are all these people doing? They have just finished building a high wall around their city. "Now, Ezra," they said, "bring out God's Book and read His words to us." When Ezra opened God's Book, everyone stood up. Now Ezra has been reading a long time. Every once in a while he stops, and his helpers tell the people what God's words mean. All the men are listening. All the ladies are listening. The boys and girls are listening. They want to know what God says in His book so they can do what pleases Him.

QUESTIONS:

1. *What did the people build?*
2. *What did they ask Ezra to do?*
3. *Why do they want to know what God says in His book?*

Nehemiah 8:1-13

Queen Esther has heard some bad news. She is coming to talk to the king about it. Somebody wants to kill Queen Esther's aunts and uncles and cousins and all the rest of God's people. Now Esther knows it is not safe to visit the king if he does not want to see her. So Esther and her friends have been praying. "Lord, help the king to be kind. Help him want to save the lives of all God's people." And now here comes Queen Esther, dressed in her pretty clothes. The king will see her. He will hold out his golden stick to her. That means, "Queen Esther, I'm glad to see you. What can I do to help you?" Do you think God heard Queen Esther's prayer?

QUESTIONS:

1. *Who is the queen?*
2. *Why is she visiting the king?*
3. *What will the king do with his golden stick?*
4. *What does that mean?*

Esther 5:1-3

This man is Ezekiel. He is far from home. He doesn't know it yet, but God has some work for him to do right where he is. Ezekiel was out by the river when the wind started to blow. It looked like a storm was coming. But, no, this was more special than a storm. Ezekiel saw clouds and lightning. Then God let him see angels too. And wheels. And a rainbow. Best of all, he even saw the Lord Himself, looking like a king on a throne. Ezekiel looked and looked. But now he is listening. He is hearing God's voice talking to him. God is saying, "Go to My people. Tell them My words." And Ezekiel will do just what God says.

QUESTIONS:

1. What is the man's name?
2. Is God in this far-away place?
3. What special things does God show Ezekiel?
4. What does God tell Ezekiel to do?

Ezekiel 1:4-28—2:1

aniel is talking to the king. The king had a strange dream. His dream was *so* strange, he was sure it meant something special. So he asked his wise men, "What did I dream? What does my dream mean?" But the wise men couldn't tell him. Daniel said, "Please let me have a little time. Then I will tell you." Daniel hurried home. He asked his three friends to pray. "Please, Lord, tell Daniel what the king dreamed. Tell him what the dream means." And God did. Now it's morning. The king says, "Daniel, can you tell me what I dreamed?" Daniel says, "No. No man can do that. But God can. God knows what you dreamed, O king. He knows what your dream means. God wants you to know some things that are going to happen." Then God will help Daniel tell about the dream. And the king will be happy.

QUESTIONS:

1. *Who is talking to the king?*
2. *What does the king want to know?*
3. *Who knows what you dream at night and think about in the daytime?*

Daniel 2:1-10; 16-29

These three men are friends. And they are all in trouble. Let me tell you about them. The king has made a big man all of gold. It shines and shines in the sun. The king said that when the music plays, everybody must bow down to the gold man. "If you don't," he said, "my soldiers will throw you into the fire." Now the three friends love the Lord God. They know He does not want them to pray to a shining gold man. And the three friends say no. Then the king is very angry. "Make the fire hotter!" he says, "Throw those men in!" Down, down they will fall into the fire. But then something very wonderful will happen. God won't let the fire hurt them. He will send His angel to be with them. When the king says, "Come out!" they will. Their clothes won't even smell smoky. And the king will know that it was the Lord God who took care of them.

QUESTIONS:

1. *Why are the three men tied up?*
2. *Will the king throw them into the fire?*
3. *Will the fire burn them?*
4. *What will the king learn?*

Daniel 3:14-28

94

It is night time, and the king is sleeping. He is having another strange dream. He sees a big tree that goes up, up, up to the sky. Birds come to sit in its branches. People come to eat its fruit. Then, in his dream, the king hears an angel say, "Chop it down!" When the king wakes up, he will ask many wise men what the dream means. But only Daniel will know, because God will tell him. Daniel will say, "Oh, king, you are like that tree. You are a great, strong king—like the tree is tall and strong. But you won't listen to what God says. You won't think about God at all. Please start doing what is right, or the Lord will stop you from being king." For when kings or other people are proud of themselves, the Lord knows what to do. He will show the king that he is king only because God lets him be king.

QUESTIONS:

1. What will happen to the tree in the king's dream?
2. Is the king proud of himself?
3. Who tells the king what his dream means?
4. What will happen to the king?

Daniel 4:5-25

95

One day when Mary is busy in her house, an angel comes to the door. He says, "The Lord is with you." Mary is surprised. Why would he say that? The angel says, "Don't be afraid, Mary. God is pleased with you. You will have a baby." Then the angel starts to tell Mary about her baby. Mary's baby will be a boy. She will call Him Jesus. He will be king over God's people some day. And He will be God's Son. Mary says, "How can I have a baby like that?" The angel says, "God will do it. Nothing is too hard for God to do." And Mary says, "All right. If He wants me to be the mother of His Son, I will."

QUESTIONS:

1. *Who is standing at the door?*
2. *Whose house is this?*
3. *What good news does the angel tell Mary?*

Luke 1:26-38

It is night time, and Joseph is having a dream. Joseph is a man who loves God very much. He loves Mary too. Maybe he was thinking about Mary when he went to sleep. In his dream, Joseph sees an angel, and the angel talks to him about Mary. "Joseph, let Mary be your wife and take care of her. She will have a baby boy. He will be God's Son. Call Him *Jesus*." Now the name *Jesus* means "somebody that saves." The angel says, "Call Him *Jesus* because *He will save* His people from their badness." When Joseph wakes up, he will do what God's angel says. He will take Mary to be his wife, and they will name the baby *Jesus*.

QUESTIONS:

1. *Who is having a dream?*
2. *Where did the angel come from?*
3. *What does the name* Jesus *mean?*
4. *Why does God want the baby named Jesus?*

Matthew 1:18-24

97

And here He is—Mary's baby and God's Son, Jesus. God has sent Him. He will grow up and take away people's badness. But what is God's Son doing in this place? Mary and Joseph are far away from home. The motel is full of people. Nobody has said, "Come stay at our house." So Mary and Joseph are staying in a kind of barn. Mary didn't want to put her new baby on the floor, so she wrapped Him up and put Him to bed in the manger box. A manger is the box the donkeys eat out of. Right now only Mary and Joseph know who their baby is—the Son of God.

QUESTIONS:

1. *Who put the baby in the manger box?*
2. *Who is the Baby Jesus?*
3. *Why is God's Son sleeping in a bed like this?*

Luke 2:4-7

Who is talking to King Herod? They are wise men from far away. They are looking for Baby Jesus. They say, "Where is the new baby king? We saw His special star. We have come to bring Him presents." But King Herod doesn't want there to be any new baby king. Herod wants to be king all by himself. So he says, "Go find the baby. Then come back and tell me where He is. I want to bring Him presents too." Now Herod does not want to bring the baby presents. He wants to kill Him. But don't worry. God always knows what to do. God will help the wise men find Jesus. Then He will tell them not to go back to King Herod. And Jesus will be safe.

QUESTIONS:

1. *Who wants to bring Jesus presents?*
2. *Who wants to kill Him?*
3. *Who always knows what to do?*

Matthew 2:1-12

Look at this angry king. It is Herod, and he is *very* angry. The other day he sent men to Bethlehem to look for Baby Jesus. He told them to come back and tell him where Jesus is. Herod wants to kill the baby. He waited and waited. But they didn't come back. "Those men fooled me," he is saying. "But I know what to do. I'll kill *all* the baby boys in Bethlehem." Here he is telling his soldiers what to do. It will be a very sad time in Bethlehem. But God won't let the king's soldiers get Jesus. God has work for Jesus to do. God will make sure that Jesus grows up. Someday Jesus will save His people from their badness. And that's what God wants.

QUESTIONS:

1. *Why is the king so angry?*
2. *Will the soldiers get Baby Jesus?*
3. *Who is stronger than the king?*

Matthew 2:16-18

See, the king's soldiers did not hurt Jesus. Here He is far away and safe with His mother and Joseph. This is what happened. One night Joseph had another dream. In his dream he saw God's angel. He heard the angel say, "Get up. Take the baby and His mother. Run away to the land of Egypt. Stay there till I tell you to come back. Herod is going to look for the baby. He wants to kill Him." Aren't you glad God knows everything? He knew what Herod would try to do. Aren't you glad Joseph likes to obey God? Right away he got up. He woke up Mary. They got the baby ready. And off they started while it was still night. And now here they are, coming into Egypt, where they will be safe.

QUESTIONS:

1. Who told Joseph what the king would do?
2. What did the angel tell Joseph to do?
3. Will the bad king find them now?

Matthew 2:13-14

101

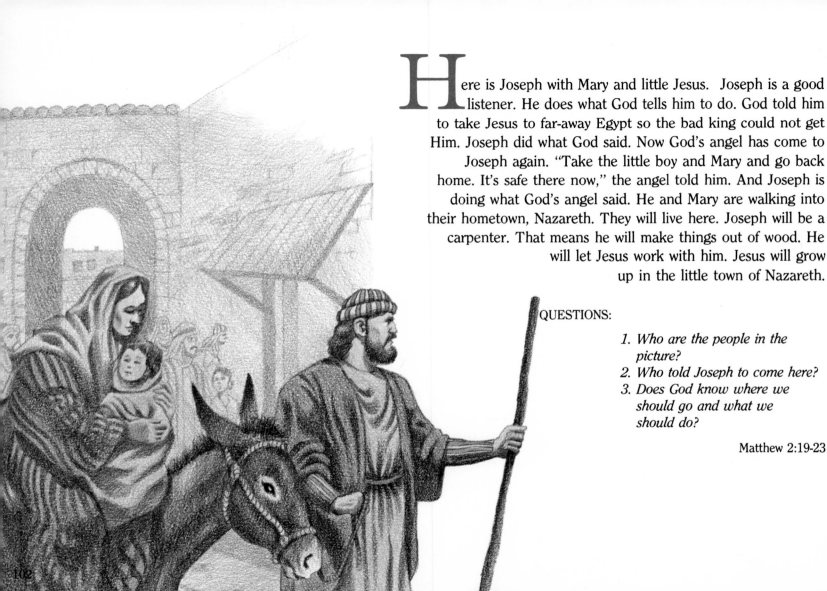

ere is Joseph with Mary and little Jesus. Joseph is a good listener. He does what God tells him to do. God told him to take Jesus to far-away Egypt so the bad king could not get Him. Joseph did what God said. Now God's angel has come to Joseph again. "Take the little boy and Mary and go back home. It's safe there now," the angel told him. And Joseph is doing what God's angel said. He and Mary are walking into their hometown, Nazareth. They will live here. Joseph will be a carpenter. That means he will make things out of wood. He will let Jesus work with him. Jesus will grow up in the little town of Nazareth.

QUESTIONS:

1. *Who are the people in the picture?*
2. *Who told Joseph to come here?*
3. *Does God know where we should go and what we should do?*

Matthew 2:19-23

102

esus is bigger now. He is twelve years old. Which one is Jesus? He is in the temple-church. That is where His Father, God, wants Him to be today. He is talking with the wise men who work there. He is listening to them talk about God. He is asking them questions. Soon Mary and Joseph will come in. Mary will say, "We have been looking for You!" And Jesus will answer, "Didn't you know that I would want to be in My heavenly Father's temple-church?" Then Jesus will say good-bye to the men. He will go home with Mary and Joseph. And He will do what they say.

QUESTIONS:

1. *Where is Jesus in this picture?*
2. *What is He doing with these men?*
3. *When Joseph and Mary come, what will Jesus do?*

Luke 2:41-51

103

Now Jesus is grown up. He is going for a long walk in the wild country. He will be there many days. He will not have friends to talk to. He will not have food to eat. The bad angel Satan is there. Satan thinks this is a good time to make Jesus do something wrong. Satan talks to Jesus about how hungry He is. Satan talks to Jesus about being king of the whole world. Satan talks to Jesus about doing a hard trick so people will like Him. But Jesus is stronger than Satan. He wants to do what pleases God. He won't do what's wrong, not now or ever. So Jesus says no to Satan. No, no, no, no, no. And after a while Satan goes away.

QUESTIONS:

1. *Where is Jesus going?*
2. *Who will come to talk to Him?*
3. *What will Satan want Jesus to do?*
4. *Will Jesus do what is wrong?*

Luke 4:1-13

Is this Jesus? No, this man is John. Long ago God said He would send a man to get things ready for Jesus to come. And John is the man. John lives out in the wild country. See how the wind blows his hair? People will come out to hear him talk. "Somebody special is coming," John will say. "He is more important than I am." John will be talking about Jesus. People will say, "Maybe John himself is the Special One that God is sending." But John will shake his head. "No, no. Not me. I only tell about Him. God's Special One is coming. Get ready for Him."

QUESTIONS:

1. *Is this Jesus?*
2. *Where does John live?*
3. *Who comes out to hear John talk?*
4. *What does John tell the people?*

Matthew 3:1-5

Almost every day people come out to the wild country to listen to John. He talks about God. He talks about the Special One God is sending. One day John looks up and sees these men coming. He can tell that they are from the temple-church. They ask John, "Who are you? Who are you, to be preaching this way? Are you God's Special One?" John will say, "No." "Well, then, are you somebody else important?" John will say, "No." "Then who *are* you?" John will say, "I am just a voice. I'm just telling you to be ready for that Special One when He comes."

QUESTIONS:

1. *Where is John preaching?*
2. *What do these men want to know?*
3. *Is John the Special One from God?*
4. *Who is?*

John 1:19-23

106

I t is a sunny day. Many people have walked down to the river. They want to see John. They want to hear him talk about God. They want to hear him talk about the Special One who is coming. All at once John looks up. He sees Jesus coming. John says, "Look! Look! There He is. There is the man I've been talking about. There is God's Special One. He will take away the badness of the whole world." All the people are looking at Jesus now. Some of the people must think, *What does John mean?* Some of the people must think, *How can one man take away the badness of everybody?* But Jesus can do it because He is God's Son.

QUESTIONS:

1. *John sees somebody coming. Who is it?*
2. *Does John tell anybody? Who?*
3. *What does John say Jesus will do?*

John 1:29-34

Soon the sun will go down. Jesus was walking home. Two men followed Him. One man was Andrew. The other man was his friend. They wanted to know Jesus better. Soon Jesus turned around. He saw the two friends. Jesus asked, "What do you want?" Andrew said, "Teacher, where are You staying?" Jesus didn't say, "I'm too busy to talk with you." He didn't say, "I'm too tired to talk to you." In the picture Jesus is saying, "Come along, and you'll see where I'm staying." "Good," Andrew and his friend say. They will go with Jesus. They will talk with Him the rest of the day.

QUESTIONS:

1. *Who was following Jesus?*
2. *What did Jesus ask them?*
3. *What will Jesus and the men do the rest of the day?*

John 1:35-39

Remember Andrew? (He's the one in the blue coat.) "Brother Simon, brother Simon!" Andrew said one day. "We have found Him. We have found God's Special One. I'll take you to Him." Well, Andrew's brother wanted to see God's Special One, so he started off with Andrew. In this picture, Andrew has brought Simon to Jesus. Simon is glad to see Jesus. And Jesus is glad to see Simon. He knows all about Simon. He knows Simon will someday be one of His best friends and helpers. Jesus says, "Simon, you are going to have a new name. Your new name will be Peter."

QUESTIONS:

1. *Who found God's Special One?*
2. *Who has brought his brother to Jesus?*
3. *Who is getting a new name?*
4. *What is it?*

John 1:40-42

Here is John, still out in the wild country. Today some of John's friends have come to see him. "John," they say, "we have heard some news. Remember Jesus, the man you said is God's Special One? Well, we heard that all the people are going to Jesus now instead of to you!" John's friends think that news might make John sad. But it doesn't. John says, "That's good. I told you I am not the Special One from God. I was just getting things ready for Him. God's Special One is Jesus. People will go to hear Jesus now. That's the way it should be. And I am happy."

QUESTIONS:

1. *Who came to see John one day?*
2. *What did they tell him?*
3. *When John heard the news, was he sad or glad?*

John 3:26-30

One day Jesus and His friends took a long walk. They went up the hills and down the hills. After a while Jesus sat down beside this well to rest. His friends walked into the town to buy lunch. While they were gone, this lady came to get some water. Jesus knows who she is. He knows everything. But the lady does not know who Jesus is. They talk about water. They talk about her family. They talk about what God is like. They talk about the Special One God promised to send. Then Jesus says, "I'm that Special One." The lady will leave her water jar. She will hurry back into the town to tell people Jesus is there. "Come," she will say. "Come and see Him."

QUESTIONS:

1. *Why is Jesus resting?*
2. *Do we know this lady's name?*
3. *Does Jesus know her name?*
4. *Will Jesus tell her He is God's Special One?*

John 4:6-29

Remember the lady with the water jar? Here she is, back again, listening to Jesus. Can you find her? But who are these other people? When the lady hurried back to town she said, "Come see a man who told me everything I ever did! Can He be God's Special One?" All these men, and more too, have come out to see Jesus. They are listening to Him talk about God and about what God wants. Many of them believe He is God's Special One because of what the lady said. Many more believe He is God's Special One because they have heard Him themselves. They ask Jesus to stay for a while, and they say to the lady, "Now we have heard Him with our own ears. We know that He is the Special One who has come to take away the badness of the world."

QUESTIONS:

1. *How did these men find out about Jesus?*
2. *What is Jesus doing?*
3. *What do the men know about Jesus?*

John 4:28-30, 39-42

What is Jesus doing in this picture? He is in a church-house. He has been reading from God's Book. He has been reading a part that talks about God's Special One coming. He tells the people about how He has come from God. But the people in the church-house don't want to hear that. They don't think Jesus has come from God at all. They say, "Humph. This is just Jesus. We know His family. He's nobody special." The longer they listen to Jesus, the angrier they get. In a minute they will jump up and take Jesus outside. They will want to throw Him down the hill. But God won't let them do it.

QUESTIONS:

1. *What is Jesus doing?*
2. *Why are the men so angry?*
3. *Is Jesus really God's Special One?*
4. *Do the men think He is?*

Luke 4:16-30

113

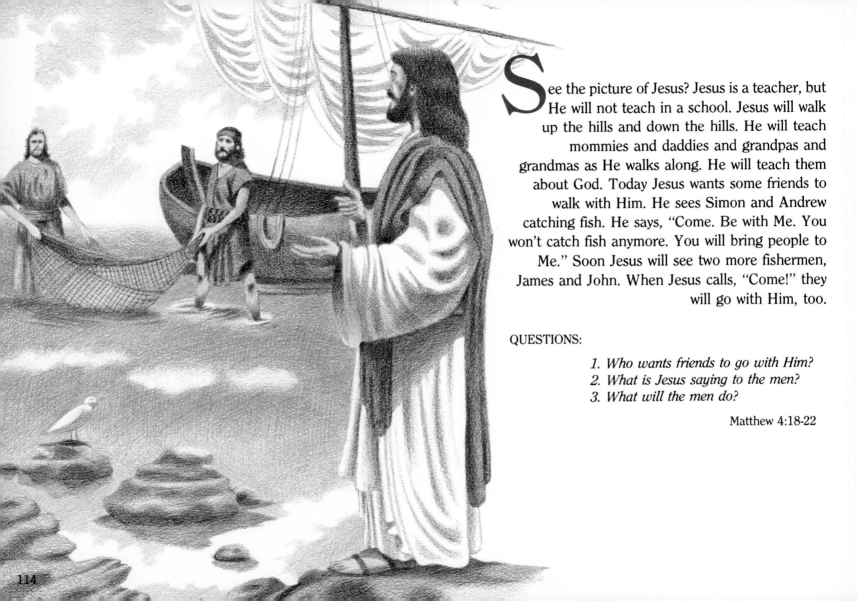

See the picture of Jesus? Jesus is a teacher, but He will not teach in a school. Jesus will walk up the hills and down the hills. He will teach mommies and daddies and grandpas and grandmas as He walks along. He will teach them about God. Today Jesus wants some friends to walk with Him. He sees Simon and Andrew catching fish. He says, "Come. Be with Me. You won't catch fish anymore. You will bring people to Me." Soon Jesus will see two more fishermen, James and John. When Jesus calls, "Come!" they will go with Him, too.

QUESTIONS:

1. *Who wants friends to go with Him?*
2. *What is Jesus saying to the men?*
3. *What will the men do?*

Matthew 4:18-22

Jesus is at Simon and Andrew's house today. This lady is Simon's wife's mommy. She has a fever. She doesn't feel like working. She doesn't feel like walking around. As soon as Jesus got there, the family said, "Lord, Mother is very sick. Would You please help her?" Now Jesus is beside her bed. He holds her hand. He makes the fever go away. Right away she feels like getting up. She is well. She will start working. Soon there will be a big crowd outside. (See the people at the window?) All the people who have sick boys or girls or mommies or daddies will bring them. Jesus will go out and make them all well. Jesus is stronger than any kind of sickness. Jesus is God's Son.

QUESTIONS:

1. *Why is this lady in bed?*
2. *Who came to visit in her house today?*
3. *What is Jesus doing?*

Luke 4:38-40

115

Every day Jesus was busy. He talked to people about God. He did kind things for people who needed help. Today Jesus met this man. We don't know his name. We just know that he was sick all over, and the doctor couldn't make him better. The man was so sick that other people wouldn't even let him come close. But Jesus let him come close. The man is saying, "Lord, if You just want to, You can make me well." And Jesus' kind heart feels sorry for the man. He will touch him. He will say, "I do want to. Be well." As quick as a wink the sick man will be better all over—his arms, his feet, his whole body. Do you suppose he will say thank you?

QUESTIONS:

1. *Why won't people let this man come close to them?*
2. *Why did Jesus let him come close?*
3. *What has just happened to the man?*

Mark 1:39-42

The man in the pretty coat is Matthew. Matthew has nice things. Matthew works with money every day. He gets to buy a lot for himself. But Matthew has not been a good man. Most people don't want to go to Matthew's house. Today Jesus came walking along. He saw Matthew sitting and working with his money. He knew how bad Matthew was. But Jesus said, "Matthew, come and walk every day with Me." And can you guess what happened? Matthew decided to leave his money. He will go along with Jesus. Matthew hasn't been a good man, but Jesus wants to make him good. Jesus loves even the people that other people don't like.

QUESTIONS:

1. *What is Jesus saying to Matthew?*
2. *What will Matthew do?*
3. *What does Jesus want to do for bad Matthew?*

Luke 6:27-28

17

What is going on at Matthew's house? Matthew is having a big dinner for Jesus. Look at the people coming. And we can't even see them all. Lots of these people are men like Matthew. They work with money every day. They take too much for themselves, just as Matthew used to do. Soon some men from the temple-church will look in. They will say to Jesus, "Why are You having dinner with all these bad people?" But Jesus will say, "It's the mommies and daddies and boys and girls who do wrong that need Me to change them." God's Book, the Bible, says that *all* mommies and daddies and boys and girls have done wrong. So everybody needs Jesus. You too.

QUESTIONS:

1. Whose house is this?
2. What will Matthew do for Jesus?
3. Who needs Jesus?
4. Do you need Him?

Luke 5:29-32

What is going on here? And why are so many sick people lying around that pool of water? They all think that if they get into the water at the right time, they'll get better. The man Jesus is talking to has been sick for a long, long time. Jesus knows that. Jesus knows what the man's sickness is too, and He knows why the man is sick. Jesus says, "Do you want to be well?" The man says, "Oh, my. I have nobody to help me. I've tried to get into the water. But somebody always gets in first." Jesus says, "Get up. Pick up the mat you are lying on. And walk." Right away his sick legs get strong. Right away he will stand up. He will fold up his mat, and he will walk. The man who has been sick a long, long time will be well. Jesus will do it.

QUESTIONS:

1. *Do we know the man's name?*
2. *Who does know all about him?*
3. *Who will make him well?*

John 5:1-3, 5-9

Something wonderful has just happened to this man. Let me tell you about him. When Jesus came into the church building a while ago, this man was there. Something was wrong with his hand. He couldn't pick up anything with it. He couldn't carry anything in it. Other men were there too. See them? They didn't care that the man's hand was sick. They were watching Jesus. They hoped Jesus would do something wrong so they could complain about Him. Jesus told the man to come up front. Then Jesus looked around. He was unhappy that the peoples' hearts were so hard. They didn't care if this poor man was sick or well. Then Jesus said to the man, "Stretch out your hand." The man did, and now his sick hand is well and strong.

QUESTIONS:

1. *Where is this story happening?*
2. *Why is this man so happy?*
3. *What makes Jesus sad?*

Mark 3:1-6

Where is Jesus today? Is He getting ready to take a boat ride? No, He is getting ready to talk to these mommies and daddies and grandmas and grandpas and friends. These people heard that Jesus makes sick eyes see. They heard He makes sick ears hear. They heard He makes sick legs strong. So big crowds of people walked up the hills and down the hills to get here. The sick ones tried to touch Jesus. They pushed so close that nobody else could see. So Jesus will sit in the little boat where everybody can see and hear. He will tell them what God is like. He will tell them what God wants people to do. Jesus loves people. Jesus has a kind heart. God is like that, too.

QUESTIONS:

1. Is Jesus going for a boat ride?
2. What is He doing in this boat?
3. Can you think of one kind thing Jesus did?

Mark 3:7-10

122

It is night time. See the darkness? Other people are in bed now. It is a quiet time to talk to God. Jesus will pray to God all night long. We don't know what He is praying about. But we do know what He will do tomorrow. He will call to Him the big group of people He has been teaching. He will choose some of them—Simon Peter, Matthew, Andrew, James, John, and enough more to make twelve. He wants these twelve men to be with Him. Then He will send them out to teach other people. Sometimes we call these twelve men Jesus' "disciples." That means learners.

QUESTIONS:

1. *What is Jesus doing?*
2. *How long will He pray this time?*
3. *What will He do tomorrow morning?*

Luke 6:12-16

The man in the doorway is a soldier. One of his helpers is sick. A while ago the soldier sent some men to Jesus. He said, "Ask Jesus please to come and make my helper well." Soon somebody ran into the soldier's house. "He's coming! He's coming! Jesus is coming!" The soldier said, "Oh, my. That's good. But maybe Jesus won't feel right about coming into my house. Tell Him I'm not good enough. Tell Him to just say a word where He is, and I know my helper will be better." So here are the soldier's men. They are telling Jesus. Jesus is pleased that the soldier believes in Him. And when the friends get back to the soldier's house, the helper will be all well.

QUESTIONS:

1. *Who wants Jesus to come and make his helper well?*
2. *Who says he is not good enough to have Jesus in his house?*
3. *Who is pleased that the soldier believes in Him?*

Luke 7:2-10

123

own the road go Jesus and His friends. Lots of people are walking with them. They come to a town. And what is this? A big crowd of sad-looking people meets them. A young man has died. He is his mother's only boy. Jesus sees her crying, and His kind heart feels sorry. He says, "Don't cry." Jesus will come up close. He will talk to the dead young man, and the young man will hear him. "Young man, get up!" The young man will sit up. He will start to talk. And Jesus will give him back to his mother. Only God can make dead people live again. Jesus is showing the people that He has come from God.

QUESTIONS:

1. *Why is the lady crying?*
2. *What does Jesus say to her?*
3. *What does He say to the dead young man?*
4. *What does the young man do?*

Luke 7:11-17

124

How sad this man looks. He is John, one of Jesus' good friends. A bad king has shut him up in jail. John has heard something exciting. Jesus made a soldier's helper well again. Jesus made a dead young man alive again. Maybe John is thinking, *Jesus does wonderful things. Then why doesn't Jesus get me out of this jail?* So John has sent friends to Jesus to ask Him, "Are you *really* God's Special One?" Now John is waiting while his friends talk with Jesus. They will say, "John wants to know if you *really* are God's Special One." Now Jesus loves John. He will say, "You go back and tell John that people with sick eyes can see now. People who had sick ears can hear now. People who had sick legs can walk now." Yes, Jesus is God's Special One—even if He does let His friend John have trouble for a while.

QUESTIONS:

1. *Who is this man?*
2. *Who put him in jail?*
3. *What does John want to know?*

Luke 7:18-23

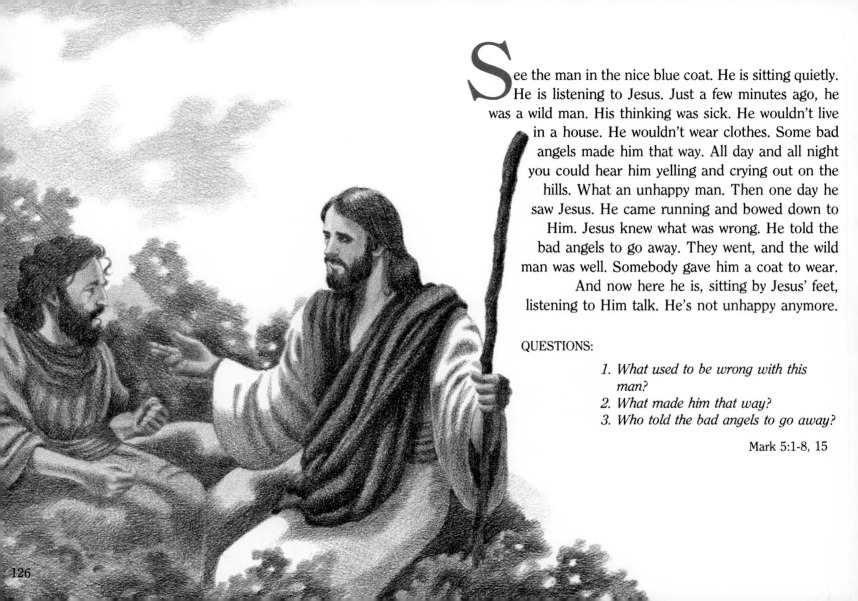

See the man in the nice blue coat. He is sitting quietly. He is listening to Jesus. Just a few minutes ago, he was a wild man. His thinking was sick. He wouldn't live in a house. He wouldn't wear clothes. Some bad angels made him that way. All day and all night you could hear him yelling and crying out on the hills. What an unhappy man. Then one day he saw Jesus. He came running and bowed down to Him. Jesus knew what was wrong. He told the bad angels to go away. They went, and the wild man was well. Somebody gave him a coat to wear. And now here he is, sitting by Jesus' feet, listening to Him talk. He's not unhappy anymore.

QUESTIONS:

1. *What used to be wrong with this man?*
2. *What made him that way?*
3. *Who told the bad angels to go away?*

Mark 5:1-8, 15

R emember that wild man? Jesus made him well. Here he is. It is time for Jesus to get into the boat and go to another place. The man who was wild is saying to Jesus, "Please, oh, please, let me go with You." But Jesus kindly answers. "No. You go back home. Let your family see that you aren't wild anymore. Tell them what God has done for you." And the man will do what Jesus says. He will do even more. He will go through his whole city, saying, "I'm not wild anymore. The bad angels are gone. Jesus did it."

QUESTIONS:

1. *Where is Jesus going?*
2. *Who wants to go along?*
3. *What does Jesus tell him to do instead?*

Mark 5:18-20

I s this lady trying to stop Jesus? No, she is doing something else. This little lady has had a bleeding for a long time. She has gone to many doctors. But is she better? Not a bit. Then she heard about Jesus. She thinks, *If I can just touch Jesus' coat, I know I'll get well. I won't even need to ask Him.* Here she is reaching out and—there! She touches His coat, and she feels well right away. But Jesus will turn around. "Who touched My coat?" His friends will say, "Lots of people. Everybody is pushing." But Jesus knows the lady is there. He will look right at her. She will tell Him why she touched Him. She will say, "I am well now." Is the lady better because Jesus' coat is magic? No, she is well because she believed He could make her well. And Jesus will send her home, happy.

QUESTIONS:

1. Why is the lady touching Jesus' coat?
2. What will Jesus do for her?
3. Was it really the coat that made the lady well, or was it Jesus?

Mark 5:24-34

This man is Herod. Herod is the bad king who put John in jail. Does he look like a happy man? For a while Herod liked to hear John talk about God. Then John would say, "You must do what is right." But he wouldn't. Not King Herod. At last the king said, "Kill John!" And they did. Now the king has been hearing about Jesus. People everywhere are saying, "Jesus makes sick eyes see! He makes sick legs walk! How can Jesus do that? He must really be John, alive again." "Yes," Herod says. "Jesus must be John—the one I killed—alive again." But Jesus is not John. Jesus is Jesus, God's Special One. Someday the king will see Jesus. But will he say, "Lord, I've been bad. Please forgive me"? No, not Herod.

QUESTIONS:

1. Is this a happy king?
2. Is he a king who loves God?
3. Why is this a sad story?
4. Why else?

Mark 6:14-16

129

It is church day. Look at the big crowd of people who have come to listen to Jesus teach. Some grandpas and grandmas are here. Some daddies and mommies are here. Some aunts and uncles are here. They are all listening carefully. Do you suppose they are thinking, *Jesus must be God's Special One. He makes sick people well. He makes dead people alive!* No, they aren't thinking that at all. They are thinking, *Humph. We know who this is. It's just Jesus. We know Mary, His mother. We know His brothers and sisters. How can He do such special things?* They don't believe Jesus has come from God at all. They sit and listen to Jesus talk. Soon they will go home. But they won't know who Jesus really is.

QUESTIONS:

1. *Where is Jesus teaching?*
2. *Are the people listening to Him?*
3. *Do they think Jesus is God's Special One?*

Mark 6:1-6

hy are Jesus' friends listening so carefully today? See Jesus talking to them? He has some work He wants them to do. They have heard Him teach people about God. They have seen Him make sick people well. They have seen Him help people who had bad angels bothering them. Today Jesus is saying, "Now, you do it." That sounds hard. But Jesus' friends don't need to worry. God will be right with them to help the sick people. And God is stronger than all the bad angels. God will make sure they have enough to eat, too—and houses to sleep in. When we do what pleases Jesus, we don't need to worry about anything.

QUESTIONS:

1. *Who are these men Jesus is talking to?*
2. *What is He telling them?*
3. *Will they do what Jesus says?*
4. *Who will take care of them?*

Luke 9:1-6

I t is church day. These people have been in the church house, listening to Jesus. But they are not just walking home. These people will not come back. What can be the matter? Well, one day when they were hungry, Jesus gave them all the bread and fish they wanted. They hoped He would do it again. But Jesus wants them to think about God more than about food. He wants them to think about forever things. In the church house He talked about belonging to God and living forever with Him. The people don't want to hear that. But Peter and John and Andrew and Matthew and many more—see them?—they won't go away. They know Jesus is God's Special One, and they want to be with Him.

QUESTIONS:

1. *Where was Jesus teaching today?*
2. *What did He talk about?*
3. *Will some people go away from Jesus?*
4. *Who wants to be with Him?*

John 6:48-69

esus and His twelve helpers are taking a long walk. On the way Jesus asks them, "Who do people say that I am?" His friends say, "Oh, some people think You are John, alive again. Other people say You are one of God's men who lived long ago." Then Jesus says, "But you—who do *you* say that I am?" Peter answers before anybody else. Peter is saying, "You are the Christ—God's Special One from heaven." Jesus is pleased. He says, "Peter, it's God who made you know that."

QUESTIONS:

1. *Who are these men with Jesus?*
2. *What does Jesus ask them?*
3. *Who does Peter say Jesus is?*
4. *Who do you say Jesus is?*

Matthew 16:13-20

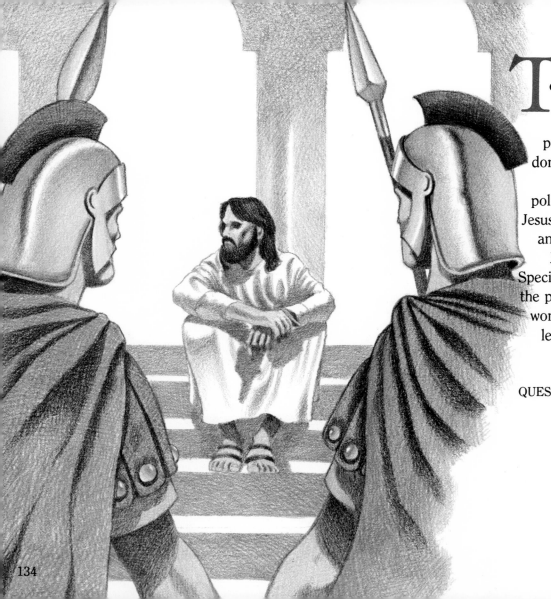

Today Jesus is sitting in the temple-church. He is teaching about God, and many people are listening. But who are these men? They are policemen. The leaders don't like Jesus. They don't want the people to listen to Him. So they have sent the policemen to get Him. The policemen listen to Jesus talk too. After a while Jesus will stand up. He will say in a big voice, "If anybody is thirsty for God, he should come to Me!" Some men will say, "Jesus surely is the Special One from God." Other men will say, "No, the police should take Him away." But the police won't take Jesus away. They will go back to the leaders. They will say, "Nobody ever, ever has talked the wonderful way Jesus talks."

QUESTIONS:

1. *Where is Jesus teaching?*
2. *Who sent the policemen?*
3. *Will the policemen take Jesus away?*

John 7:32-52

This morning Jesus was sitting in the temple-church. All at once in came these angry men. They pushed this lady to the front. "She is a bad one," they told Him. "People should throw stones at her. What do you say?" Now Jesus knows everything the lady has done. He knows she has done a bad thing. But Jesus knows He soon will die to take away this lady's badness. Jesus will talk to the angry men. After a while they will go away. Jesus will quietly say to the lady, "You may go too. And don't do wrong again." You see, Jesus loves even the people who do not do very nice things.

QUESTIONS:

1. *Where are Jesus and the other people?*
2. *What do the angry men say about the lady?*
3. *Will they throw stones at her?*

John 8:2-11

Something important is happening in this picture. All these men are friends of Jesus. He is giving them some work to do. "Go two by two," Jesus is saying. "Go to the little towns and the big towns. Tell people that I am coming to their town soon." So Jesus' friends will go. Will everybody be glad to hear that Jesus is coming? No, some people will be glad to hear the news. But some won't. Jesus' friends will have to come back to Him and say, "We're sorry, Jesus. The people in this place and that place—they wouldn't listen to us." And that's the way it is today. Not everybody is glad to hear that Jesus is God's Son. But some people are. They say, "What good news!"

QUESTIONS:

1. *What is Jesus telling His friends to do?*
2. *Will they go?*
3. *Will everybody be glad to hear that Jesus is coming?*

Luke 10:1-11

The lady in the blue dress lives in this house. Her name is Martha. Today she has invited Jesus and the twelve disciples for dinner. That is a lot of people to cook for. But Martha wants to do it. See how hard she is working in the kitchen? She wants her sister, Mary, to come and help. But Mary likes to be with Jesus and listen to Him talk. Pretty soon Martha will come in and say, "Lord, tell my sister to help me!" But Jesus will say, "Martha, Martha, don't be so worried." You see, Mary is doing something even more important than fixing dinner for Jesus. She is spending time with Him and listening to what He says.

QUESTIONS:

1. *Who came to visit today?*
2. *Who is working in the kitchen?*
3. *Who is listening to Jesus?*
4. *What is even better than fixing a nice dinner for Jesus?*

Luke 10:38-42

Jesus has been talking with God. We call that praying. When He finished, one of His friends said, "Lord, teach us to pray." So Jesus is telling His friends what they should talk to God about. "Thank God that He is good," Jesus says. "Tell Him about anything you really need. Tell Him when you have done something wrong. Ask for help so you won't do wrong next time. And pray for other people, not just for yourselves." God likes to hear boys and girls and mommies and daddies pray that way.

QUESTIONS:

1. *What do we call talking to God?*
2. *What did Jesus' friends ask Him?*
3. *What are some things you can pray about?*

Luke 11:1-13

Once upon a time there was a rich farmer. His garden was big. It grew so much wheat and other things that the farmer started to worry. Here he is, looking at his field. "What shall I do?" he is saying to himself. "I don't have a barn big enough for all this wheat. I know. I'll tear down the barns I have. I'll build bigger barns. Then I can eat and drink and be happy. I'll have all I need for a long time." But God will say to the rich farmer, "You are foolish. Tonight you will die. Then all your good things won't help you at all." Some people are like the rich farmer. They spend their time getting and building and having fun. They don't think at all about getting ready to be with God. Jesus says they are foolish.

QUESTIONS:
1. *Does the farmer have a good garden?*
2. *What does he think he will do?*
3. *What does he forget to do?*

Luke 12:16-21

139

Jesus is teaching His friends today. He is saying, "Don't worry about having enough food to eat. Don't worry about having enough clothes to wear." In the picture some birds are flying over their heads. "Think about the birds," Jesus says. "Birds don't plant gardens. But God has a way of feeding them." Then Jesus will look at His friends. He will say, "You are much more important than birds. Don't you think God knows how to give you what you need?" The men will think, *Jesus is right. God loves us. He will give us what we need.*

QUESTIONS:

1. *Where are Jesus and His friends today?*
2. *What is Jesus saying about birds?*
3. *Will God take care of Jesus' friends?*
4. *Will He take care of you?*

Luke 12:22-24

Is this lady happy, or is she sad? Something very special has just happened to her. Let me tell you about it. Jesus was in the church house. Lots of other people were there too. Then in came this lady. She was walking all bent over. Long ago one of Satan's bad angels had given this lady a sickness. Other people could look up and see the blue sky. But not this lady. Her head was down all the time. When Jesus saw her, He knew what had made her sick. He said, "Woman, be well." Then He touched her, and right away her back was straight. Here she is standing up and looking at Jesus and smiling a big smile. "Thank God!" she is saying. "Thank God!"

QUESTIONS:

1. *Where are Jesus and the lady?*
2. *Why is the lady smiling?*
3. *What is she saying?*
4. *What could you thank God for?*

Luke 13:10-16

This man is blind. He can't see anything—not people, or puppies, or flowers, or stars. He has been this way ever since he was a baby. He can't see to work, so he sits all day beside the street. He hopes somebody will put some money in his brown bowl. Soon Jesus will come along. Jesus will give him something better than money. First, Jesus will put a kind of mud on the man's eyes. Then Jesus will say, "Go, now, and wash the mud off." Maybe the man won't understand, but he will do what Jesus tells him anyway. When he washes, his blind eyes will be well. His neighbors will say, "Who is this? It looks like the blind man. But it can't be. This man can see." The man will say, "I'm the one! Jesus put something on my eyes. He said to go and wash. I did, and now I can see! Jesus did it!"

QUESTIONS:

1. *What does the man hope people will put in his bowl?*
2. *Why doesn't he work?*
3. *What will Jesus do for him?*
4. *What has Jesus done for you?*

John 9:1-11

The blind man is happy that he can see again. Look at his big smile. He is telling the leaders how it happened. But the leaders are not happy. They don't care that the blind man can see now. They are angry. They don't want people to think that Jesus has come from God. They tell the blind man, "Just thank God that you can see. We know this Jesus is not a good man!" But the man who had been blind says, "Oh, my. All I know is that I couldn't see before, and now I can. Jesus opened my eyes. Jesus is from God, or He couldn't do that."

QUESTIONS:

1. *Why is this man so happy?*
2. *Are the other men happy too?*
3. *What is the blind man telling them?*

John 9:13-33

Here he is again—that blind man Jesus made well. He has been looking at things all day. He knows now what his friends look like. He knows now what trees look like. He knows now what houses look like—and streets and babies and blue sky. Now Jesus has found him looking around. Jesus says, "Do you believe in God's Special One?" "Who is He?" asks the man. Jesus says, "You are looking at Him. He is talking to you." The man will say, "Lord, I do believe." You and I haven't seen Jesus yet. Do you believe in Him anyway?

QUESTIONS:

1. *What has the blind man been looking at today?*
2. *Who made His eyes well?*
3. *What will Jesus say to him?*
4. *What will the man say to Jesus?*

John 9:35-38

This man is not Jesus. This man is a shepherd. He takes care of sheep every day. They are *his* sheep. He knows their names, and they know him. The sheep like to hear his voice. They go with him when he calls them. The shepherd knows sheep get hungry. He finds green grass for them to eat. He knows sheep get thirsty. He finds nice water for them to drink. He knows sheep get tired. He lets them lie down. He doesn't let any lion or wolf or bear get them. He would even die to help his sheep. He is a good shepherd. Jesus is like a shepherd. We are like sheep. Jesus takes care of us. And one day Jesus died because we needed somebody to take our badness away.

QUESTIONS:

1. *What are the sheep doing?*
2. *Who gives the sheep what they need?*
3. *Who is your Good Shepherd?*

John 10:24-29

This little woman has ten shiny round pennies. She likes to wear them around her head. A while ago she counted her money. "One, two, three, four, five, six, seven, eight, nine—nine! I've lost one!" Now the little woman didn't say, "Oh, well, I have nine left." No, she thinks the lost one is important. She lighted her lamp so she can see better. She has been sweeping all the corners. She hasn't found the lost penny yet. But she will. (Do you see it?) When she finds it she will tell her friends. "Be happy with me. I have found the piece of money I lost." There are lots of people in the world. But God thinks each one of us is important.

QUESTIONS:

1. *How much money did the lady lose?*
2. *What will she do when she finds it?*
3. *Are you important to God?*

Luke 15:1-10

146

You can tell that this will not be a very happy story. Look at the angry faces. The leaders are saying bad things today. They are saying, "We must do something about Jesus." They know Jesus made that blind man's eyes well. They know He made that dead young man live again. And the lady who was bleeding—they know He made her better too. They know that. But they do not want to believe that Jesus is God's Son. They are saying, "Let's kill Him!" That is sad. Some people today have heard what Jesus can do. But they don't want Him either. Their badness has made their hearts hard.

QUESTIONS:

1. *Are these men Jesus' friends?*
2. *What has made their hearts so hard?*
3. *Have you heard about Jesus?*
4. *Do you want Him?*

John 11:47-53

147

The man in the big chair is a judge. He is supposed to help people by telling them what is right and what is wrong. But this man is not a good judge. Another man wants to take away something this lady has. She is asking the judge to help. But the bad judge won't help. The lady will come back another day. She will ask for help. But the bad judge won't help. So she will come back still another day. At last the bad judge will say, "I guess I will help this lady just so she will stop bothering me." And he will. Listen—the judge was bad; he helped the lady just to get rid of her. But God is good. Keep asking Him for what you need. He will give you the help you need because He loves you.

QUESTIONS:

1. *What does the lady want?*
2. *Is this a good judge?*
3. *Why will the judge help the lady?*
4. *Why will God help you when you pray?*

Luke 18:1-8

One day Jesus told a story. He said two men went into the temple-church to pray. And here they are. Both men are just like everybody else in the world. They need God to forgive them for not doing right. But this man in the black coat doesn't think he needs God to forgive *him*. When he prays, he says, "God, thank You that I am not like other people. I do many good things. I don't cheat people. I'm not bad like that man over there." The other man is too ashamed even to look up. See him? He just prays, "God, I've done wrong. Please forgive me." Jesus said that's the man God forgave. And the man went home happy.

QUESTIONS:

1. *Who told a story about these two men?*
2. *What did both men need?*
3. *Which man did God forgive?*
4. *Why?*

Luke 18:9-14

Jesus is walking up the hill to the big city. He knows that the leaders there will kill Him. His friends are afraid. See how slowly they walk. Soon Jesus will call them close. He will say, "When we get to the city, the leaders will take Me to the king's helper. His soldiers will hit Me. They will make fun of Me. They will put Me on a cross to die." Then Jesus will say, "After three days, I will be alive again." Jesus' friends won't understand now. But when He does come alive again, and they see Him, they will understand. Then they will say, "Jesus *told* us He would rise again. And He has. Just as He said."

QUESTIONS:

1. *Where is Jesus going?*
2. *Does He know what will happen to Him there?*
3. *What good thing does Jesus say will happen?*

Mark 10:32-34

Somebody has come to see Jesus today. It is James and John's mother. She says, "Jesus, when You are king, please say that my two boys can be the most important people in Your kingdom." When the other disciples hear that, they are angry. They would like to be important themselves. Soon Jesus will call them over to Him. He will say, "People in this world like to be important. They like to tell others what to do." Then Jesus will say, "But you are My people. Don't you try to be important. You try to help other people. Be like Me. I came into the world to help other people and to give My life for them."

QUESTIONS:

1. *What does this lady want?*
2. *Why are the other disciples angry?*
3. *What will Jesus say about being important?*

Matthew 20:20-28

151

Who can this man be? He is called Bartimaeus, and something is wrong with his eyes. Bartimaeus can't see to work. All he can do is sit beside the road and wish he could see. But today something exciting will happen to Bartimaeus. Right now he is hearing a big noisy crowd of people. Jesus is coming! Bartimaeus can't see Jesus, but somebody will tell him Jesus is there. Then Bartimaeus will start to yell, "Jesus, help me! Jesus, help me!" Will Jesus stop to help just one man? Yes, He will. Jesus will make the blind man's eyes well, and Bartimaeus will go with Jesus down the road.

QUESTIONS:

1. *What is wrong with this man?*
2. *How does he know Jesus is coming?*
3. *Will Jesus hear Bartimaeus call for help?*
4. *Will Jesus stop to help just one man?*

Luke 18:35-43

Is little Zacchaeus trying to get away? No, he has climbed up high so that he can see Jesus when He walks by. I'm sorry to tell you that Zacchaeus is not a very good man. He has money that he has taken from other people. But now here comes Jesus and a big crowd. In a minute everybody will be surprised. Jesus will stop under this tree. "Zacchaeus," He will say, "come down. Hurry. I'm going to your house." The people will grumble. "Jesus is going to visit a bad person." But Zacchaeus will say, "Jesus, I'll give back all the money I've taken from people—and even more." You see, nobody is too bad for Jesus to love. And nobody is too bad for Jesus to change.

QUESTIONS:

1. Is Zacchaeus a good man?
2. Why is he climbing that tree?
3. Will Jesus change Zacchaeus?
4. How do you know?

Luke 19:1-10

153

This is Mary—not Jesus' mother, but another Mary. Jesus and His disciples are having dinner at her house. Mary has been thinking and thinking. *What nice thing can I do to please Jesus?* So while everyone else is at the table eating, Mary comes in with this perfume. It is very, very good perfume. It cost a lot of money. Mary wants Jesus to have it because He is so important to her. She will carefully pour the perfume on Jesus' head and on His feet. That's what they did in those days. And the Lord Jesus will be pleased. He will say, "People all around the world will someday hear about what Mary has done."

QUESTIONS:

1. Is this lady Jesus' mother?
2. What is she carrying?
3. Why does she want Jesus to have it?

Mark 14:3-9; John 12:3

W ho is this? And why is he so angry? He is Judas, one of Jesus' disciples. He is at the supper table. And Mary has just put some good perfume on Jesus. Judas says, "Oh, my. What a waste! She could have sold that perfume for lots of money. Then she could have given the money to poor people." But Judas really doesn't care about the poor people. He doesn't care about Jesus. He likes money, and he wants to steal some for himself. Jesus will say, "Let Mary alone. She has done a good thing."

QUESTIONS:

1. *What is Judas saying?*
2. *Does he really want the poor people to be given money?*
3. *Does Judas love Jesus?*
4. *What does Judas love?*

John 12:2-8

Look at the donkey. Will one of these men ride on it? No, they will take it to Jesus. The Lord is waiting just outside the town. Jesus said to these two friends, "Go into the little town. As soon as you get there you will see a young donkey tied. Untie it and bring it to Me. If anybody asks what you are doing, tell him, 'The Lord needs it, and He will send it back.'" So here they are. In a minute the owners will say, "What are you doing with our donkey?" Jesus' friends will say, "The Lord needs it. He will send it back." And the owners will say, "All right." Soon Jesus will be sitting on that donkey, riding into town.

QUESTIONS:

1. Are the men stealing the donkey?
2. Would Jesus tell anybody to steal?
3. What will Jesus do with a donkey?

Matthew 21:1-7

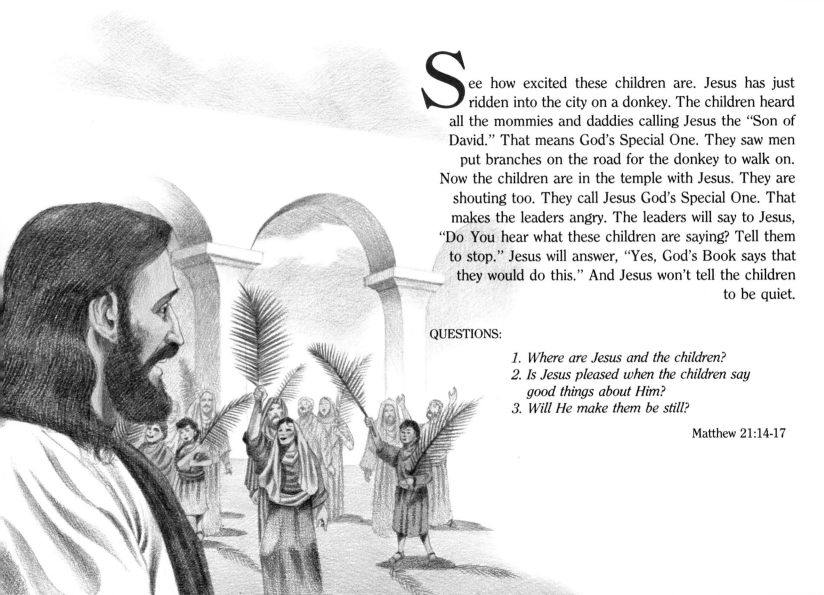

See how excited these children are. Jesus has just ridden into the city on a donkey. The children heard all the mommies and daddies calling Jesus the "Son of David." That means God's Special One. They saw men put branches on the road for the donkey to walk on. Now the children are in the temple with Jesus. They are shouting too. They call Jesus God's Special One. That makes the leaders angry. The leaders will say to Jesus, "Do You hear what these children are saying? Tell them to stop." Jesus will answer, "Yes, God's Book says that they would do this." And Jesus won't tell the children to be quiet.

QUESTIONS:

1. *Where are Jesus and the children?*
2. *Is Jesus pleased when the children say good things about Him?*
3. *Will He make them be still?*

Matthew 21:14-17

157

What can Jesus be doing? Just a while ago He walked into this part of the temple-church. He saw men selling birds. He saw people buying birds. He saw money stacked on tables. That did not make Jesus happy. He made the bird-sellers stop. He said no to the people who wanted to buy birds. Now He is upsetting the money tables. He is saying, "The temple-church is supposed to be a place to pray." But the men had made it a place to cheat and make money for themselves. Jesus is right. But the leaders won't like it when they hear what He has done. They will think hard how they can get rid of Him.

QUESTIONS:

1. *Why is Jesus unhappy?*
2. *What does God want people to do in the temple-church?*
3. *Who doesn't like what Jesus does?*

Mark 11:15-18

See how many people have come to listen to Jesus today. There are almost too many to count. The sad part is that they are *only* listening. They are not believing what He is saying. They really don't think Jesus is God's Son. He has done many things to show them who He is. Can you think of any? Did He make the blind man's eyes well? Did He make the dead young man sit up and talk? Today Jesus is telling the people that He will die. They won't understand that He will die and then come alive again. They won't understand at all.

QUESTIONS:

1. *Who is listening to Jesus teach today?*
2. *Do their ears hear Him talking?*
3. *Do they believe Jesus is God's Son?*

John 12:32-40

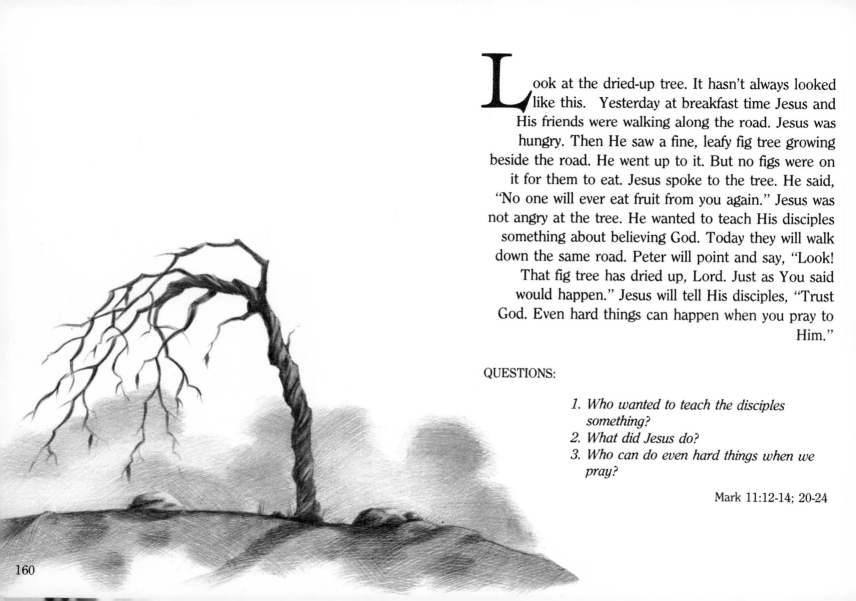

Look at the dried-up tree. It hasn't always looked like this. Yesterday at breakfast time Jesus and His friends were walking along the road. Jesus was hungry. Then He saw a fine, leafy fig tree growing beside the road. He went up to it. But no figs were on it for them to eat. Jesus spoke to the tree. He said, "No one will ever eat fruit from you again." Jesus was not angry at the tree. He wanted to teach His disciples something about believing God. Today they will walk down the same road. Peter will point and say, "Look! That fig tree has dried up, Lord. Just as You said would happen." Jesus will tell His disciples, "Trust God. Even hard things can happen when you pray to Him."

QUESTIONS:

1. *Who wanted to teach the disciples something?*
2. *What did Jesus do?*
3. *Who can do even hard things when we pray?*

Mark 11:12-14; 20-24

That thing in Jesus' hand—what is it? It's a piece of money. The bad leaders have sent men to ask Jesus if it is all right to pay money to the king. They think Jesus will be in trouble if He says yes. They think He will be in trouble if He says no. But Jesus is wise. He doesn't say yes, and He doesn't say no. He says, "Whose picture is on this money?" The men say, "The king's picture." "Then," Jesus says, "give the king what belongs to him. And give God what belongs to Him." The men are surprised at Jesus' good answer. Can you think of something that belongs to God? The Bible says even our bodies belong to Him.

QUESTIONS:

1. Who sent men to trick Jesus?
2. Who was wise?
3. Who was surprised?
4. What do you have that belongs to God?

Matthew 22:15-22; 1 Corinthians 6:19-20

These three men are Abraham, Isaac, and Jacob. They lived in the world a long time ago. Abraham, Isaac, and Jacob do not live here now. But they are alive. They live with God. One day Jesus was talking about heaven. He said things in heaven will be different, but people there will be alive—Abraham, Isaac, Jacob, Peter, Matthew, John, Mary, Martha, and you too, if you believe Jesus is God's Special One.

QUESTIONS:

1. *Who said people will be alive in heaven?*
2. *How does Jesus know what heaven is like?*
3. *Where are Abraham, Isaac, and Jacob today?*

Matthew 22:31-33

Have you ever seen a mother hen with her baby chicks? When a dangerous animal comes around, the hen spreads out her wings. She says, "Cluck, cluck, cluck, cluck." And all her babies come running. They hide under her wings and are safe. One day Jesus talked to the city of Jerusalem. He said, "You won't listen when God's men talk to you. I would like to take care of your people like a mother hen cares for her chicks. But you won't listen to Me calling you." Then Jesus said, "Because you won't come, you will have much trouble. Just like a baby chick that won't come when its mother calls."

QUESTIONS:

1. *Who wants to take care of the baby chicks?*
2. *Who wanted to take care of the people in Jerusalem?*
3. *Who wouldn't listen to Jesus calling them?*

Matthew 23:37-39

163

A minute ago Jesus and His friends were in the temple-church. The temple was a beautiful place. It was made of shiny wood and big white stones and gold. On the way out, the disciples said to Jesus, "See! What wonderful stones. What wonderful buildings." Now Jesus is telling them what will happen to these pretty buildings. "Some day," He says, "every one of these stones will be broken down." That means that someday the beautiful temple-church will be broken down. Look at the mens' faces. They must be thinking, *How can that happen? Surely that won't happen.* But Jesus knows, for Jesus is God's Son.

QUESTIONS:

1. *What did the disciples show Jesus?*
2. *Do they think the temple is big and beautiful?*
3. *Who knows what will happen to the temple?*

Luke 21:5-6

164

You will never guess why Peter and John are following that man. Let me tell you. It is Passover time. At Passover time everyone fixes a special supper. But Jesus and His friends are not at home. Where will they eat the special supper? Jesus said to Peter and John, "Walk into the city. You will meet a man carrying a jar of water. [See the jar?] Follow that man. When he goes into a house, you go in too. The man who lives in the house will show you a room all ready for us. You can make our supper ready there." So here go Peter and John, following the man with the water jar. He will lead them to the right house. And they will make supper ready.

QUESTIONS:

1. *Who told Peter and John to follow that man?*
2. *Where is the man going?*
3. *Does Jesus always know just what to do?*

Mark 14:12-16

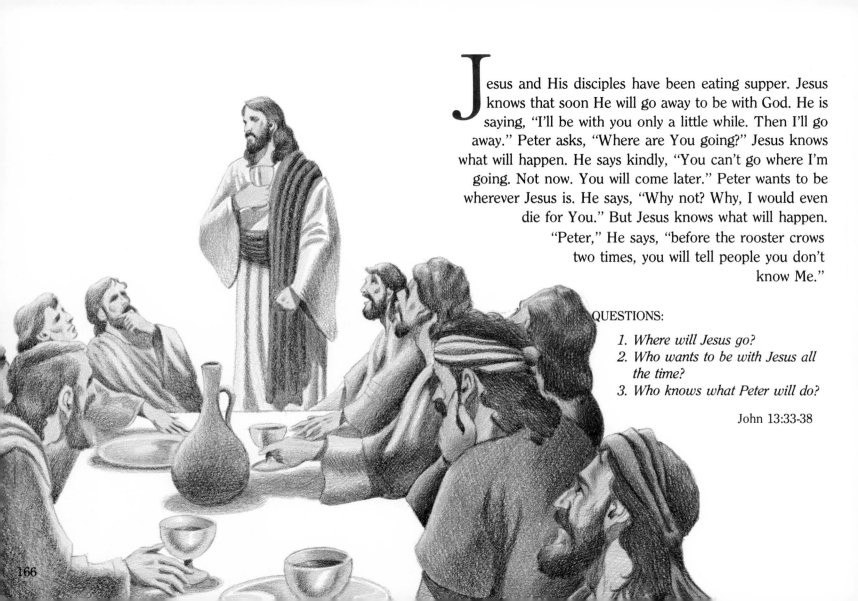

Jesus and His disciples have been eating supper. Jesus knows that soon He will go away to be with God. He is saying, "I'll be with you only a little while. Then I'll go away." Peter asks, "Where are You going?" Jesus knows what will happen. He says kindly, "You can't go where I'm going. Not now. You will come later." Peter wants to be wherever Jesus is. He says, "Why not? Why, I would even die for You." But Jesus knows what will happen. "Peter," He says, "before the rooster crows two times, you will tell people you don't know Me."

QUESTIONS:

1. *Where will Jesus go?*
2. *Who wants to be with Jesus all the time?*
3. *Who knows what Peter will do?*

John 13:33-38

ook at Jesus' disciples. They are listening to Jesus. But they can't understand what He means. He is talking about going away to be with God. The disciples will say to each other, "What does He mean? He says that in a little while we won't see Him. Then He says that in a little while we *will* see Him. What does He mean?" Jesus knows what people are thinking. He knows His friends don't understand. So He will say, "You are going to be very sad, because I will die. But I will see you again. I won't stay dead. Yes, you will be sad," Jesus will tell them. "But when I am alive again, you will be happy."

QUESTIONS:

1. *Who is in this picture?*
2. *What will make them sad?*
3. *What will make them happy?*

John 16:16-22

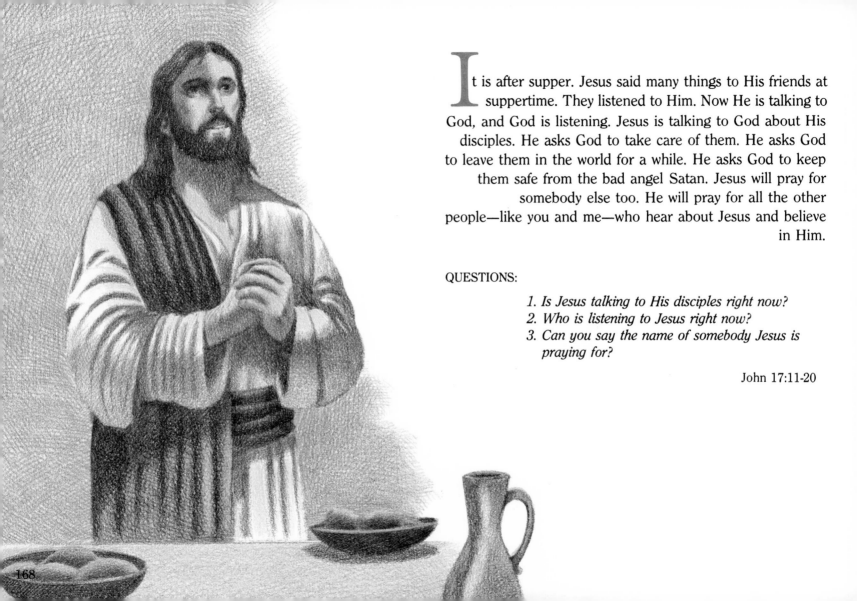

It is after supper. Jesus said many things to His friends at suppertime. They listened to Him. Now He is talking to God, and God is listening. Jesus is talking to God about His disciples. He asks God to take care of them. He asks God to leave them in the world for a while. He asks God to keep them safe from the bad angel Satan. Jesus will pray for somebody else too. He will pray for all the other people—like you and me—who hear about Jesus and believe in Him.

QUESTIONS:

1. *Is Jesus talking to His disciples right now?*
2. *Who is listening to Jesus right now?*
3. *Can you say the name of somebody Jesus is praying for?*

John 17:11-20

168

Can you tell what time it is? Yes, it is night. Supper is over now. Jesus and His friends sang a thank-you song to God. Now they are walking to a garden of trees. Jesus likes to come here. It is a good place to pray. He is saying, "You sit here and wait. I will go over there and pray." He will take Peter and James and John with Him. He knows that soon God will put on Him all the badness of all the world's people. That makes Him feel very sad. But Jesus won't say no. He will pray, "Father, whatever You want is all right."

QUESTIONS:

1. *Where are Jesus and the disciples?*
2. *What will Jesus do here?*
3. *Why is Jesus sad?*
4. *What will Jesus tell God?*

John 18:1; Mark 14:32-42

169

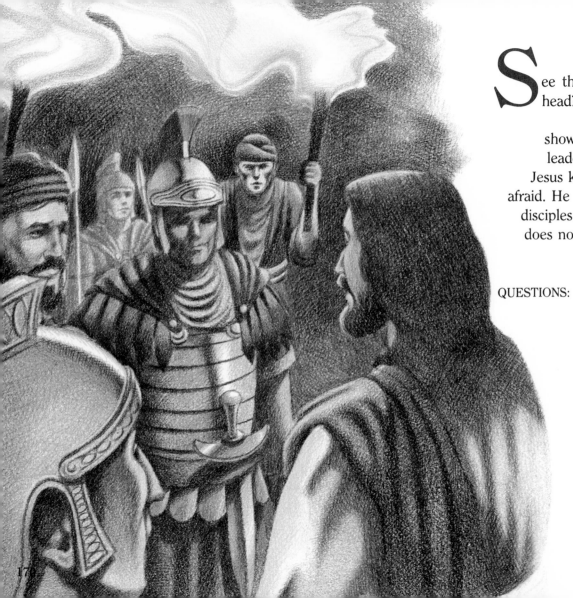

See the man with the green cloth around his head? It is Judas, one of Jesus' disciples. What is Judas doing with those soldiers? He is showing the soldiers where Jesus is. The bad leaders will give Judas money for doing that. Jesus knows what will happen. But Jesus is not afraid. He comes out to talk with the soldiers. The disciples are afraid. They all run away. But Jesus does not run away. He stays, because He knows that is what God wants.

QUESTIONS:

1. Who is bringing the soldiers?
2. Who is it the soldiers want to catch?
3. Why doesn't Jesus run away?

John 18:2-4; Mark 14:50

See what the leaders have done now. They have tied up Jesus. And He has let them do it. They are taking Him up the steps to see the king's helper. And He is letting them do it. This morning the leaders talked together. They said, "We want to kill Jesus. But we aren't allowed to. Let's say that Jesus has done something very bad. Then the king's helper will have Him killed." What a sad, wrong thing to do. But Jesus will let them do it. He loves us. He will die for us so that someday we can live in heaven with God.

QUESTIONS:

1. Do the leaders like Jesus?
2. Where are they taking Him?
3. What is Jesus going to do for us?

Matthew 27:1-2

171

The big man is the king's helper. A minute ago he was talking to Jesus. He listened carefully to what Jesus said. Now he is outside talking to the angry leaders. The king's helper will tell them Jesus has done nothing wrong. Nothing wrong. Nothing wrong at all. Somebody else knows that Jesus has not been bad. God, looking down from heaven, knows that Jesus has not been bad. Not ever. Jesus has always done just what pleases God, and He always will.

QUESTIONS:

1. *Who is the man who is talking?*
2. *What is he telling the leaders?*
3. *Has Jesus done anything wrong?*

John 18:28-38

The king's helper is sitting in his big chair. He says to
the people, "Shall I let Jesus go?" He knows Jesus has
not done anything wrong. But the people get very noisy. They
yell at the king's helper. "Don't let Jesus go! Let Barabbas
go!" Now Barabbas is a robber. Besides that, Barabbas is in
jail for killing someone. "Let Barabbas go free!" the people
yell anyway. The king's helper says, "Then what shall I do with
Jesus?" The people shout, "Let Him die on a cross!" The
king's helper should say no, but he doesn't. He says, "All
right. Jesus must die, and Barabbas will go free."

QUESTIONS:

    1. Who says, "Shall I let Jesus go"?
    2. Who says, "No. Let Barabbas go"?
    3. Why is Barabbas in jail?
    4. What will happen to Jesus?

                    Mark 15:6-11, 15

This is a sad picture. The leaders don't want Jesus. The king's helper has said He must die. The soldiers put a prickly crown on Jesus' head. Now He is carrying His cross to the dying place outside the city. Jesus does not have to let people do these things to Him. If He asked God, many angels would come to save Him. But Jesus won't ask for help. He will die on that cross. He wants to die for us because He loves us. Jesus will die so that God can forgive us and make us His men and women and boys and girls.

QUESTIONS:

1. *What is Jesus carrying?*
2. *What is on His head?*
3. *Will He ask the angels to save Him?*
4. *Say the name of somebody Jesus loves?*

John 19:17

174

What a sad thing is happening in this picture. The soldiers have put Jesus on this wooden cross to die. Can you see the soldier? Can you see the leaders waving their arms and making fun? The rest of the people are just watching. But something else is happening in this picture—something is happening that only God can see. God is doing something with the badness of all the people in the world. He is putting it on His Son, Jesus. Jesus is being punished instead of you. He loves you. He is dying on the cross so that someday you can live for always with Him in heaven.

QUESTIONS:

1. *Can you see what the people are doing?*
2. *Can you see what God is doing?*
3. *What is God doing for you in this picture?*

Luke 23:35; Isaiah 53:6

175

The man is Joseph—not Mary's husband, but another Joseph. He is talking to the king's helper. He says, "Sir, Jesus has died. Please let me take Him away." The king's helper says, "All right." So Joseph will hurry back to the cross. He will take down Jesus from the cross and will wrap Him up. Close by there is a little room chopped into the rocky hill. He will put Jesus there. Then Joseph will push a big stone in front to be a door. Joseph is sad. He doesn't know that soon Jesus will be alive again.

QUESTIONS:

1. *Who is talking to the king's helper?*
2. *What does Joseph want to do?*
3. *What is the good news in this story?*

John 19:38-42; Matthew 27:60

It is early in the morning—so early it is still dark. There is the rocky hill. There is the little stone room where Joseph put Jesus. But what is happening? Someone is pushing the big stone away from the door. It is an angel! His clothes are as white as snow. He is bright like lightning! In a minute the angel will sit right down on that stone and wait. When some ladies come, looking for Jesus, the angel will say, "I know you are looking for Jesus. He died on a cross. But He is alive again. He is not here anymore. Come and see."

QUESTIONS:

1. Who is moving the stone?
2. What will the angel do next?
3. Who will come soon?
4. What will the angel tell them?

Matthew 28:2-3

177

The lady is Mary Magdalene. She thought Jesus was still dead. But here He is alive! Just a while ago Mary Magdalene was crying. She was beside the little stone room where they had put Jesus. The room was empty. Jesus was not there. She thought, *Oh, somebody has taken Him away.* Then she saw a man standing nearby. At first Mary Magdalene thought he was the man who takes care of this place. But no, it is Jesus Himself. He says her name. "Mary." And she knows who it is. She sees Him. She hears Him. Now she will touch Him. Yes, Jesus is really alive again. When Mary Magdalene finds Jesus' friends, she will say, "I have seen the Lord!"

QUESTIONS:

1. *Who is seeing Jesus?*
2. *Who is hearing Jesus?*
3. *Who will touch Jesus?*
4. *Is Jesus really alive again?*

John 20:11-18

The man talking with Jesus is one of His friends. His name is Thomas. Mary Magdalene has been saying, "I have seen the Lord." The other disciples have been saying, "We have seen the Lord." But Thomas has been saying, "*I* won't believe He is alive again. Not unless I see the places in His hands where they nailed Him to the cross." In the picture, Jesus is visiting His disciples again. He tells Thomas, "Look at My hands." He tells Thomas to touch them. Thomas sees the nail places. And Thomas says, "My Lord and my God." He knows who Jesus is, and He knows Jesus is really alive.

QUESTIONS:

1. *What is this disciple's name?*
2. *What is Jesus showing Thomas?*
3. *What will Thomas say?*
4. *What will Thomas know?*

John 20:24-29

Peter and his friends have been fishing. They were on the boat all night, but they did not catch any fish. Not even one. The sun was just about to come up when they saw Jesus on the beach. They didn't know it was Jesus, but He knew them. And He knew they hadn't caught anything. He called, "Take your fishing net and throw it out on the right side of the boat. Then you'll catch some." They did what He said, and now see all the fish they have caught. Jesus knew where the fish were. "It is the Lord!" the disciples say. When they get to shore, they will see a little fire, and fish cooking, and bread. Jesus has made breakfast for them. He knows they are hungry. "Come," Jesus says. "Have some breakfast." He knows all about us too. He knows what we need.

QUESTIONS:

1. *How long did the men fish?*
2. *How many fish did they catch last night?*
3. *Who knew where the fish were?*
4. *Who knew they were hungry?*

John 21:3-13

180

L ook at the high hill. Jesus told His friends to come to this hill. Here they are, and here He is. Jesus is going back to heaven for a while. He wants His friends to do something important while He is gone. He says they must tell people everywhere who Jesus is and how to please Him. Jesus says, "I will be with you while you do this. All the time." Jesus hasn't come back from heaven yet. But someday He will. While He is away, He wants *us* to tell other people who He is and how to please Him. He will be with us too. All the time.

QUESTIONS:

1. Where will Jesus go soon?
2. What does He tell His friends to do while He is gone?
3. If you love Jesus, what does He want you to do?

Matthew 28:16-20

O h, my, it looks like Peter and John are in trouble. The temple-church police are taking them to jail. Today Peter and John were doing just what Jesus told them to do. They were telling people, "Jesus died. But He is alive again!" Then the leaders came along. They said, "Put those men in jail!" So Peter and John will be locked up all night. In the morning the leaders will say, "All right. You may go. But don't teach about Jesus anymore. Or bad things will happen to you." Peter and John will go to their friends. Then they will all pray, "Lord, make us strong inside so we'll talk about Jesus anyway."

QUESTIONS:

1. *Who will be put in jail?*
2. *Have Peter and John been bad?*
3. *Will they stop talking about Jesus?*

Acts 4:1-31

This man is Stephen. He is one of Jesus' friends. Stephen is standing in front of the leaders. God is making Stephen strong inside. He has just told them that Jesus is God's Special One. The leaders don't want to hear that. They are getting angry. Now Stephen is looking up. God lets him see right into heaven. "I see Jesus," Stephen says. "He is standing beside God." The leaders will yell at Stephen. Then they will chase him out of the city. After that they will throw stones at him until he dies. Sometimes sad things happen to Jesus' friends. But Jesus' friends go to be with Him in heaven. And that is what will happen to Stephen.

QUESTIONS:

1. *What is Stephen looking at?*
2. *What will the men do to Stephen?*
3. *Where will Stephen go?*

Acts 7:51-60

183

The man in the green coat is soldier Cornelius. He is a good man. But he doesn't know Jesus. He gives money to poor people. But he doesn't belong to Jesus. One day God sent a shining angel to Cornelius. "Ask Peter to come," the angel said. "He will tell you something important." Now Peter has come. They will go into the house. All Cornelius's family and friends are there. Peter will say, "God was with Jesus. He went around doing good. Men killed Him. But He came alive again." All the people will believe what Peter says. Cornelius too. And then Cornelius will belong to Jesus.

QUESTIONS:

1. Is soldier Cornelius a bad man?
2. Does he need Jesus anyway?
3. Do even good people need Jesus?

Acts 10:30-48

"Good-bye, Paul! Good-bye, Barnabas! Good-bye!" Paul and Barnabas are going far, far away. See the walking stick in Paul's hand? Their friends are watching them go. The friends like Paul and Barnabas. The friends would like Paul and Barnabas to stay at home and teach them. But God said no. God has something else for Paul and Barnabas to do. God knows there are other people living in far-away places. These other people need to hear about Jesus too. They don't know He is God's Special One. They don't know He died for them. They don't know He is alive again. God wants Paul and Barnabas to tell them. And Paul and Barnabas will.

QUESTIONS:

1. *Who is going away?*
2. *Why are they going?*
3. *Where are they going?*
4. *Who wants them to go?*

Acts 13:1-3

H ere are Paul and Barnabas in a far-away place. They have never been here before. See the people? Paul has been telling them that Jesus died and came alive again. Will everybody believe what Paul says? No, everybody won't believe. But *some* will. Next week Paul and Barnabas will come back. This time so many people will come that they can't all get into the church house. Paul will talk again about Jesus' dying and coming alive. Will everybody believe what Paul says? No, everybody won't believe. But *some* will. Do *you* believe that Jesus died for you and is alive again?

QUESTIONS:

1. *Where are Paul and Barnabas today?*
2. *What are they talking about?*
3. *Who is listening?*
4. *Will some of these people believe in Jesus?*

Acts 13:44-49

This is a happy picture. All the people here love the Lord Jesus. This is Paul, in the green coat. The big boy in the orange coat is Timothy. Timothy is not very old, but he is old enough to please the Lord. Paul is saying, "Timothy, people in many places still haven't heard that Jesus came, and died, and came alive again. I am going to tell them. I want you to come along." Timothy wants to please God, so he will say yes. His mommy and grandma want to please God too. They will let Timothy go and be Paul's helper.

QUESTIONS:

1. *Do only old people love Jesus?*
2. *In this picture, who wants to please God?*
   Anybody else?
3. *Do you want to please Him?*

Acts 16:1-3; 2 Timothy 1:2, 5

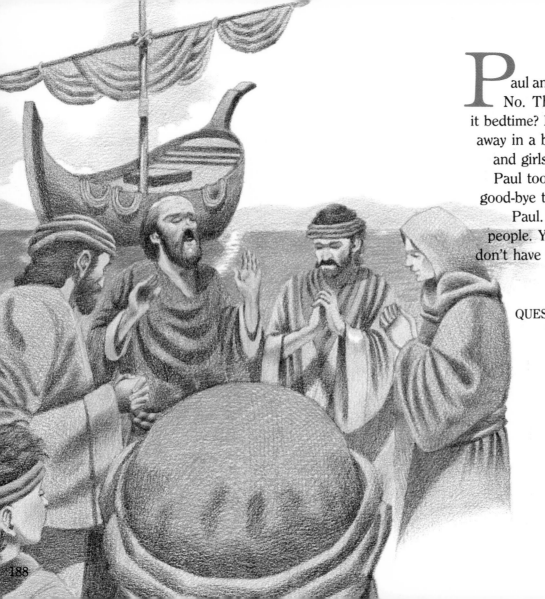

P aul and his friends are praying. Are they in church? No. They are kneeling in the sand on the beach. Is it bedtime? No. See how light it is? Paul is ready to sail away in a boat. These daddies and mommies and boys and girls love the Lord Jesus. They love their friend Paul too. They have come down to the water to say good-bye to him. They are asking God to take care of Paul. And Paul is asking God to take care of the people. You don't have to be in church to pray. You don't have to wait till bedtime to pray. You can talk to God wherever you are and any time.

QUESTIONS:

1. Who is going away?
2. How will Paul go?
3. Where are these people praying?
4. Where can you talk to God?
5. When can you talk to God?

Acts 21:3-6

Doesn't this look like fun? Paul is on this boat. But he is not taking a fun ride. Some soldiers are taking Paul far over the water. He must go to the king's city and talk to the king. Has Paul been bad? No, he has only been going everywhere talking about Jesus. The leaders still don't like that. They don't like to hear that Jesus is God's Special One. They even tried to kill Paul. But God wouldn't let them do it. Now Paul will soon be in the king's city. When he gets there, more people will hear about Jesus. Paul will tell them.

QUESTIONS:

1. Who is on this boat?
2. Where is Paul going?
3. What will Paul talk about when he gets there?

Acts 25:24-25; 27:1-2

189

See how old Paul is now. He is shut up in a house in the king's city. He has to stay inside all day. But people can come to see him. This young man is Onesimus. He used to work for a man far away. One day he took the man's money and ran off with it. Then he met Paul. And Paul talked to him about Jesus. Onesimus belongs to Jesus now. He knows that taking the money was wrong. He says he will go back home and say, "I'm sorry." He will work for the man again. Paul is saying, "I'll write a letter. You can take it with you. I'll tell the man you believe in Jesus now."

QUESTIONS:

1. *Who is the old man?*
2. *What wrong thing did Onesimus do?*
3. *Who helped Onesimus know Jesus?*
4. *What will Onesimus do now?*

Philemon 9-16

190

One day Paul thought, *I am shut up in this house. I can't walk to far-away places anymore. But I still want to teach God's people about the Lord Jesus. I want to teach them how to please God. What shall I do?* God knew what to do. He made Paul think about writing letters. He will help Paul know what to say. But Paul's eyes were sick. He couldn't see to write a letter. God knew what to do. God gave Paul friends to do his writing for him. Here is one of those friends. Paul is telling him what to say. And the man is writing down Paul's words. Today people can still read Paul's letters. They are in God's Book, the Bible. When you are a little older, you can read them too. All by yourself.

QUESTIONS:

1. Who made Paul think of writing a letter?
2. Who helped Paul know what to say?
3. Who gave Paul a helper to write for him?
4. Where are Paul's letters today?

Romans 16:22; Ephesians 1:1; Colossians 4:18

191